The Fourth Generation

a personal story of heartache and humour 1885-1985

Carole McCall is a former Civil Servant and Business Woman who has worked as a Life Coach, NLP Trainer, Psychotherapist and Hypnotherapist for many years. Working in the United Kingdom, Ireland, Spain and America she has helped many people to solve their own problems. This book is the story of how four generations of women in her own family survived against the odds to a background of the changing decades. She is a grandmother to seven small children and lives in Tunbridge Wells with her husband and a small white dog called Stella.

The Fourth Generation

a personal story of heartache and humour

1885-1985

Carole McCall

Arena Books

First published in 2014 by Arena Books

Arena Books
6 Southgate Green
Bury St. Edmunds
IP33 2BL

www.arenabooks.co.uk

Distributed in America by Ingram International, One Ingram Blvd., PO Box
3006, La Vergne, TN 37086-1985, USA.

Carole McCall
     The Fourth Generation *a personal story of humour and heartache 1885-1985*

British Library cataloguing in Publication Data. A catalogue record for this
Book is available from the British Library.

ISBN-13   978-1-909421-44-8

BIC classifications:- BTP, BGB, BGXA.

Printed and bound by Lightning Source UK

Cover design

By Jason Anscomb

Typeset in
Times New Roman

Dedicated

to

**Kathryn, Charlotte, Wendy, Lisa, Irene
And Catholine**

Glossary of leading persons featured in this book and their relationship with the author

Mona –mother

Hester - grandmother
Hannah - great grandmother
Gillian - sister
Miranda - daughter
Amy, Beth, Jane - aunts
Alexandra - paternal grandmother
Violet, Anna, Dorothy, Gloria - great aunts
Laura – Grant's mother
Viola – Grant's grandmother

Grant-husband

Murray - Father
Theo – son
James – son
Harry – brother
Frank jnr, Ned, Michael, Jeffery, Sonny, Simon, George - uncles
Frank snr - Hester's husband
Hubert - Alexandra's husband
Malcolm - Gillian's husband
Cedric, Arthur, David - great uncles
Francis – Grant's father

Foreword

There are no exceptions and therefore there are no choices. This book is about the choices people make; the limitations we set for ourselves and the possible solutions we never stand by because we assume there are none. Universal words include every, never, must, always.

Why do we obey the rules because those in authority say so, and what are they? Are the rules and boundaries we set for ourselves much stronger than the rules that other people set for us?

Why is our individual map of the world different to everybody elses? We are each unique as we are the only person in the world who has had that particular upbringing, education and life experience.

This is the personal story of four generations of English women between 1885 and 1985: their lives, their loves, their heartbreak and their joy. This is the story of why they made the choices they did. It is also the story of all of us throughout the generations against the background clamour of the outside world. My grandmother and great grandmother both died just before my wedding. Consequently they were real flesh and blood figures in my life.

Hannah was born in 1885, ethereal with beautiful green eyes she stood 4'10" tall. She ran away and left her child Hester with her Victorian parents-in-law when her husband went to America to make his fortune.

Hester was born in 1905 and was Hannah's oldest daughter. She was the mother of eleven children: powerful, outspoken and determined. The only characteristics she shared with her mother were her height and her green eyes. The day of her 16-year old son's funeral she walked home in the snow to find that a neighbour had dropped her 1-year son. He had been taken to hospital with a fractured skull. She turned around and ran all the way back to the hospital.

Mona was born in 1925 and was Hester's oldest daughter. Tall, blonde and slender she had nothing in common with her mother except her green eyes. Private, ferociously clever and bored with childcare she preferred cleaning and reading: the more complex and historical the book the better.

THE FOURTH GENERATION

Carole was born in 1950 and was Mona's oldest daughter. Dark haired, green eyed, relentlessly cheerful she was determined to be helpful from childhood. She was a feminist, loyal wife, ambitious mother and conscientious employee. Living with a lifelong illness but determined that only her husband would know. She never wanted anyone to feel sorry for her. She was too busy trying to answer the question: Can women have it all? Here are some useful pointers to consider:-

*Choice is better than no choice.

*If you always do what you have always done you always get what you always got.

*If what you are doing is not working do something else.

*There is no failure only feedback.

*You cannot not communicate.

*The meaning of communication is the response you get.

*People have all the resources that they need.

*The map is not the territory.

*People's maps are made of pictures, sounds, feelings, tastes and smells. People respond to their maps of reality not reality itself.

CHAPTER 1
Together At Last

"For goodness sake concentrate when I shout push" yelled my diminutive grandmother to her five strapping, blonde sons .She was as wide as she was tall and nobody even the vicar dared argue with her.

This was a very musical family and so my mother's brothers were assembled by their mother to push her precious piano across the garden to the church hall. The ancient but lovingly polished piano was stuck in the mud, in the Boxing Day downpour, and everyone was red faced with exertion. Hester's oldest daughter Mona was getting married in two hours and there were still so many things to be done.

The austerity of the immediate post-war years was beginning to lose its grip. However reality for many working families of that era was "mend and make do"

My parents wedding in 1947 was very much a family affair. The slim young bride and the dashing marine were finally getting married. The family lived next door to St Christopher's Church in Manchester and the whole congregation had been invited. The flowers that had been grown by Mr Griggs amongst his precious vegetables were used by Mrs Malty and her daughter to dress the church.

Mona, by that time a skilled dressmaker, had fashioned her three sister's bridesmaid's dresses out of cream silk. Miss Brookes, whose fiancé had not returned from the First World War, donated the lace she had saved from her own trousseau for Mona's dress.

The wedding breakfast, made by Hester and her friends, was to be served in the in the church hall. Ladies arrived with arms full of ham, chicken, fish and salads of all variety. Everyone had contributed food because Hester was very much respected in the community. Mona carried a large bunch of lilies and stephanotis that the local greengrocer had donated.

Once Mona was ready and her mother declared herself satisfied they were finally ready. Frank in his grey suit escorted his daughter down the aisle. Father and daughter were very alike private, quiet and reserved not a word was exchanged between them as they waited outside the church.

The ceremony proceeded and the reception was remembered by all who attended. The groom sang Perry Como's "They say it's Wonderful" to his bride and with her lovely soprano voice Mona managed a few bars of "Personality "by Johnny Mercer but that ground to a halt because she was so nervous. Her father was persuaded to give a rendition of "Gypsy" by the Inkpots.

Coincidentally I met a member of the Inkpots in New York when he was in his 90s. He was dressed in a wonderful royal blue suit and black shoes .He was singing away to his heart's content and I stopped to throw a dollar in his royal blue bowler hat. I was so entranced by his life story that I was late for my meeting!

At 6 pm when the festivities were drawing to a close Hester stood at the bottom of the stairs with Murray whilst Mona ran upstairs to put on her grey gabardine going away outfit. When she shouted "I'm decent" he was allowed to go all the way upstairs in order to escort her all the way downstairs.   As far as Hester was concerned there was to be no "dilly dallying" in her house even by people so recently married.

A neighbour had lent them a car as a wedding present and they were off to Southport. Murray was very happy as this was to be the first night his wife had ever spent in his arms.

Murray had learned to drive in the marines. He said that you were asked if you could drive and if you said "yes" they gave you a licence. The marines training must have been adequate as he is still driving in his 90s.

When they returned home the next day Mona's heart sank and she felt very unhappy. Home was to be an old house near Manchester City Football Ground with her mother-in-law, miles away from her precious family.

 Of course the fact that City football matches were only two minutes' walk away meant that my father would have lived in that house forever. He was also a good football player and a game and a pint were his Friday night treat. In common with most men of his age and situation, football and beer were the staples of his social life.

Years later I was talking to my mother about her life and I said to her "You must have been really excited about being married" She thought for a few moments whilst looking deeply into my eyes then she said" I am not like you I am just not built for excitement" My own daughter said something similar to me years later only she ended her sentence with a peal of laughter "Let's face it Mum you get excited when the cake you have put in the oven rises."

CHAPTER 2
When I Fall in Love

Mona and Murray were the perfect couple. From the day they were married she was determined to make sure his life was perfect. She cooked his favourite meals, put out his freshly pressed clothes every morning, polished his shoes and never, ever argued with him.

Their favourite song was "When I fall in Love" by Nat King Cole. Mona had a pink and white jewellery box with a beautiful ballerina that twirled around and around that played the song. They would dance around the kitchen to this music oblivious to whoever was there.

She was on the outside the perfect post-war housewife but In fact deep down she was very different. Ferociously clever and very private she spent her time cleaning and reading serious tomes. She cleaned until her fingers were raw as if it was a punishment. She read anything and everything educational. We were the only house in the neighbourhood that took the *Manchester Guardian*.

Mona and Murray had been introduced at a family party when they were both 16 and had been inseparable ever since. Murray had been asked to change a light bulb and he had dropped it on her head by accident. In the ensuing commotion whilst her head was being examined and the glass tidied up he said "She looked at me with those beautiful green eyes and I fell head over heels in love" She was dreadfully embarrassed but secretly though he was very handsome.

However her mother Hester was not very keen on the relationship at first. She knew Murray's mother Alexandra and considered that she was "a little relaxed and casual in her attitude to the important things in life". The attributes she lacked were primarily to do with housework, especially cleaning, cooking, relationships and religion.

However Murray's good looks, smart appearance and the fact that he was adored by all her younger children won her over. Their marriage was a story of true love and lasted until the day she died.

So on the day I was born in in 1950 in Prestbury, Cheshire I arrived early in the morning and I was ....well I was I guess an interloper in their perfect relationship. There is a proverb that states "The children of lovers are orphans" and I think it is really true.

Chubby, rosy cheeky and cheery were some of the adjectives used to describe me that day. My mother Mona was fragile. She weighed less than 6 stones and I was a big baby that took a long time to arrive. Murray said he looked at me and said" My goodness Mona, she is going to be bigger than you are by the time she is 2 years old"
I guess I must have heard because I do not ever remember a day in my life that I did not feel responsible for and very sorry for my mother.

Mona was the oldest girl of 11 children and they were similar to many families in working class Manchester but there were two big differences. They had at their head a matriarch Hester who was only 4ft 10 in. but ruled them with a rod of iron and secondly they were all very clever.

The oldest son in the family Frank had been a scholar at Chethams School of Music. He died of diphtheria at 16 years old and Hester lived the rest of her life through the pain of that loss.

The war had just started and Mona had just had a baby boy. Her husband Frank and her eldest son Frank junior had been admitted to the isolation hospital with diphtheria. It was snowing the day she set off to walk to the hospital to see them as the buses were not running. She left the baby Simon with a neighbour as he was too young to be looked at by the older children.

When she got to the hospital she was taken into a room to be told Frank had died. She flew to her son to console him on losing his father, who had been lying in the next bed. To her horror it was her husband Frank who was sitting up in bed with tears streaming down his face. She fell to the floor with the pain of losing her son and never ever forgave her husband for living when her beautiful boy had died.

The day had not finished with Hester. When she finally arrived home hours later it was to be told by her friend, Muriel, "Mrs Jones tripped up the step and has dropped the baby on the concrete and he was unconscious for a while. The doctor has been to see him and thinks it's a fractured skull so he has taken him to hospital".

Hester never even took her coat off she turned on her heel and stepped out again into the snow. Thankfully the baby did survive and became a very successful banker.

By the time I came along Hester's youngest son Sonny was five years old and the apple of her eye, but she had given birth nine times in the intervening fifteen years.

My grandmother Hester was a powerhouse dominating all around her. Her husband Frank was quiet and studious and looked much younger than he was. When she met people for the first time they always assumed Frank was her son. This caused Hester to become apoplectic with range. Frank did try to grow a moustache to try and look older but it made absolutely no difference!

Neither of my maternal grandparents was raised by their own parents. Frank their first child was born when they were both seventeen years old.

My diminutive great-grandmother Hannah gave birth to Hester herself when she was only 20 years old and recently married to William 21, only child of strict Victorian parents.

Hannah was born in 1885 to a young mother and an older father. Her father was 60 years old when she was born. Her mother was very poorly giving birth and became an invalid. By the time Hannah was eleven years old she was responsible for most of the housework.

Domestic duties for women at that time were very arduous. Hannah's father had a bad chest and so dust in the air was a problem. It was mostly coal dust from the fires and the factories. Everything had to be wet dusted and clothes and bed linen washed every week. It was all scrubbed and then boiled in a zinc tub. Curtains had to be taken down and washed every fortnight. Hannah was heard to remark that she hated her raw, red hands. As soon as she was able she secured employment in a milliners shop and it was there that she caught William's eye.

The young man quickly became bored with family life and he had heard lots of stories from his friends about the land of opportunity across the sea. William decided to go to America to seek his fortune on RMS Caronia and left his young wife and baby with his parents.

Nine million people emigrated to America in the first decade of the 20th century. Most people went because they saw a chance for a better life.

Hannah was very pretty with blonde hair down to her waist and the most beautiful almond shaped green eyes. (She never cut her hair and wore it braided round her head into her 80s).She loved clothes and the style of the day suited her. With her smaller frame and diminutive stature 4ft 10ins narrower dresses and smaller hats were made for her.

Left alone and being young and impressionable she fell madly in love with Frederick an older married man who owned the local dress factory. By all accounts he was very handsome and charming. They ran away in the middle of the night leaving all behind them. It was a terrible scandal and William was called back from America but his wife would not return. Fred and Hannah settled by the sea and had four more children who never knew their mother was still married to William.

William was heartbroken but he was consoled by an older lady in the neighbourhood. They set off for America and had four children of their own who never knew their father was still married to Hannah.

That left Hester to be raised by elegant, elderly Victorians who treated her like a china doll. She was dressed in the fashion of the day in velvet and lace and never allowed to play. No-one ever said "No" to her or was allowed to express an opposing opinion to hers and flew into terrible rages that no-one could control and this continued through her life.

CHAPTER 3
Hester's Companion

Hester had a maid and companion called Clara who went everywhere with her and saw to her every need and was very often the butt of Hester's spoiled ways.

Much later in life Hester discovered that Clara had in fact been her aunt. Her grandmother had never known that she was the unacknowledged child of her grandfather and a local woman of the night. It was a recipe for much heartache. Hester was very spoilt and unworldly and Frank was studious and had been raised by maiden aunts as his mother had died giving birth.

When it was discovered that Hester was pregnant Frank had to leave his education and get a job to support his family. He rarely spoke to anyone because he always had his nose in a book and he wrote with beautiful copper plate handwriting all his life.

They were allowed to be married, as these families were both very religious, but they were not allowed to live together as they were considered to be too young.

They were allowed to see each other on supervised visits but somehow she became pregnant again, with my mother and so they set up home in 1925.In the next 15 years she had 11 babies:- Frank, Mona, Ned, Michael, Jeffrey, Jane, Beth, Amy, Sonny, Simon, and George.

These seven boys and four girls were all blonde with green eyes and impeccably behaved. There were expected to be studious and all went to highly academic schools.

Although frank and Mona had seven sons, not one of them had a son and so the Bradbury name died out.

However they knew what trouble awaited them if there were any reports of misdeeds from the formidable neighbourhood ladies.

Times were very hard and food was in short supply when they were all small but when the war came along in 1940 their house was bombed out. They were all panic stricken and one neighbouring house and family were wiped out completely. In the shelter they counted of all their children. When they discovered that one daughter was missing, Frank had to climb back into the rubble and rescue Jane who had been left behind. She was deaf and had not heard the sirens.

After the blitz the majority of children from the cities were sent to the countryside for the duration of the war and that included all my aunts and uncles.

> I've packed my clothes, my Sunday best
> There is no room for all the rest,
> I have packed my memories in my head
> At night I'll share them with my ted,
> I've left home, my own bedroom,
> I've left the smell of mum's perfume,
> I've left my mum, she had to stay,
> I wish that she was here today,
> I've left my bike my pride and joy,
> I could not bring my favourite toy,
> I left my friends and all I know
> I wish I did not have to go.

This is from an anonymous poem describing evacuation from a child's viewpoint. However my family were very fortunate and had a better experience than some other children.

They took care of the animals, ate fresh food and slept in comfortable beds. They walked to school through lovely countryside and on the whole had a very positive experience.

An interesting fact emerged from their years away. Whilst the sisters missed their home and parents the experience of being an only child in the family made some of the older brothers resentful of their large number of siblings, when they returned.

Although the war was terrible and traumatic the benefit was that the older houses were demolished and lots of people had wonderful new homes. This was the case for Hester and Frank and good times slowly returned. In the later years there was always good food, music and lots of laughter at the many family occasions.

However, Hester could "turn on a sixpence" as the family called it. What had been great fun suddenly became darkness and you would all be in trouble.

CHAPTER 4
I Have Done all this Before

My mother had helped raise all these children and she often said "I have done all this before." There were so many stories of cleaning and child care and she really blamed her mother for what she considered was her lack of childhood. I adored her so much, but her feelings that already raised one large family coloured every aspect of my existence...

Here I was on a beautiful sunny June day in leafy Cheshire. The song everyone was singing was "Mule Train" by Frankie Lane and the children were definitely cheerier as sweet rationing had been lifted just weeks before.

Reality for me was actually that the maternity ward was an outpost of an inner city hospital and that home was a dilapidated house in a poor area of the city. My mother hated this house with a passion. She had moved there from her lovely family home with all her brothers and sisters around her when she married my father.

My other grandmother Alexandra was always calm and distracted and did not really ever think too deeply about anything. She was tall and elegant and always had what my mother considered "strange ideas". She cooked lunch and then drank the water the vegetables had been cooked in! She walked for miles every day and was always going to the coast "to take in the air".

She did not give a fig for convention and considered house work to be "just pointless". She came from a family where convention was all but her parents had died when she was young and she was raised by her sisters.

She had no luck with men in a time when respectability was all. She had had two children with her husband William: my father and a daughter Eileen who was seven years younger.

He left when my father was eight and Alexandra went to work as a housekeeper for a widower. Across town Eileen went with her but my father was sent away to school until he was fourteen years old. The school was some sort of foster care or approved school but it was never talked about. "It was the making of me and meant I was well educated and determined to succeed in life" were his only comments. However I know he never got over the abandonment.

Life in the 1950s was based on the principle that secrets were kept for life and that as long as the neighbours did not know it did not really matter what pain you suffered.

My grandmother married twice after that. The man I knew as granddad, Hubert, she had actually met on a bus coming back from Blackpool. He was very comfortable financially and they had a nice life for a while.

His adored only daughter Lillian who lived in New York heard about the wedding and was furious. She arrived on the Queen Elizabeth "a fashion plate dressed in furs and dripping with jewellery" and demanded that her father sign all his money over to her. She stayed one week and left with everything he had. They got a letter from her husband to say that she had died on the return trip and that was that. My mother was convinced she had died of anorexia and she ate nothing the whole time she was in England.

So Alexandra and Hubert lived the rest of their lives on a meagre pension. When Alexandra died at 86 she did not have a line on her face. All that vegetable juice and walks in the fresh air must have been good for something.

So you have met my family and life as it started for me as an only child with many doting aunts and uncles in 1950.

CHAPTER 5
The Affair of The Pigeons

My mother was very unhappy living in that old house in Manchester and decided that she would go back to work. Her mother-in-law had married Hubert and gone to live with him in North Manchester.

There was no problem as in those days even factory workers earned enough to keep their families on one wage. Most people lived in rented houses and the rents were low. When the war ended rationing slowly finished and food was plentiful and cheap.

THE FOURTH GENERATION

In the late 1940s, the National Insurance Act and National Health Service Act had become law, forming the key parts of the modern Great Britain welfare system. Benefits for everyone such as the Child Benefit were beneficial after the war and helped fund the 1950s baby boom.

My mother had passed her eleven plus, but along with many women and men of her generation there was just not enough money in the family for the grammar school uniform. Mona had been sent to work in the Scotch wool Shop at fourteen and really blamed her mother for not allowing her to join the Land Army. My Grandmother had stated "You are not allowed to go away. I need you here to help with all these children." My mother hated shop work because people "chattered too much"

As the war was looming in 1939 and the street lights were out she had fallen off her bicycle. She caught her wheel in the tram tracks. Not being one to complain she carried on with a broken leg until she collapsed. This story was like a knife to my heart whenever it was related as she could no longer stand for hours they had to find her a job sitting down. A neighbour suggested she apply for a job as a machinist. This was a loose term for women that spent all day making clothes.

My mother showed a real talent for this work and consequently was shown how to work in every department. She could take some tissue paper, some chalk and pins and a "nice piece of material" and make whatever you wanted.

My childhood memories are of her kneeling on the floor with a tape measure round her neck and a mouth full of pins cutting out a pattern. She made everything I ever wore up to a including my wedding dress.

My mother told me that one of the only arguments she ever had with Murray was over her going back to work and putting me in a nursery. Women had kept the country running in the war years. Now that the war was over men demanded to be back as the head of the household and provide for their families. It was seen as vaguely shameful if your wife had to go out to work as they were taking jobs away from men.

THE FOURTH GENERATION

Mona later told me that she had been to nursery along with the tradition of the 1920s that every child went to nursery at two years old. She had a fantastic memory and could remember everything about being there and considered it had done her "no harm"

The first nursery she found was spick and span which was the first requirement. Of course I have no memory of this but I am told there was an incident that meant I had to change nurseries quite soon.

A nursery assistant called Marjorie, had along with the fashion of the day put all the nappies around the fire guard to dry. In the fifties there was either hand washing or a boiler with a dolly to swish the water around. A free standing mangle got the surplus water out and there was nothing to dry them on except the fire if the weather was inclement. Unfortunately the hapless Marjorie had left the fire guard too near the fire and soon the whole place was alight.

Good fortune arrived that afternoon. The Fire Brigade got there quickly; the staff was on the ball and moved the children out in an orderly fashion. The fire happened late in the day so that the parents soon arrived to pick up their children. There were no phones in those days so everything was by word of mouth. In the 1950s people lived and worked in the same area so nobody was far away.

All the children and the staff had smoke in their eyes and on their faces but no-one needed to go to hospital. The nursery building itself fared much worse and had to be pulled down.

Mona was forced to give her job up and return to being a housewife. My Father considered it a sign and suggested she stayed at home. After I began to walk it became obvious that although I could not walk very fast I was quite determined. We lived on a road of terraced houses without much traffic.

This particular day I was standing in the hall watching people go by. The older kids played in the street and the younger kids watched from the safety of their house. From my vantage point I spied a flock of magical pigeons. I decided to go and run around with them. As it happened there was a milk float going slowly past and a neighbour who was just coming back from the newsagents rescued me from a certain squashing.

My grandfather Frank also happened to be a milkman and as soon as the offending milkman arrived back at depot he told the story of the nearly squashed child. My grandfather, who would not say boo to a goose, realised this was his only grandchild and reported all this to his wife. She duly marched round to tell my mother to do less cleaning and more children watching.

My mother found another job and another nursery that week. She also became determined to move away and when the landlord said they either had to buy the house or move away then the die was cast.

My father Murray was beginning to develop very left wing views and decided he was against property ownership. My father always stated "Once I have made a decision I never, ever change my mind." My mother secretly thought that really he did not want a debt of £200 hanging over his head.

Mona just set about making him think that her idea was his. She did in fact persuade him it was his idea to buy a house but that was not until the sixties.

CHAPTER 6
THE CRUSHED DREAM

The falling snow that was reflected in the twinkling lights of Christmas looked perfect and gave everyone a warm, cosy glow. Christmas in our house involved having lots to eat and having one excellent toy as well as your stocking. The main thing was not to be spoilt which was difficult for me as I had so many aunts and uncles. My mother kept to the same routine all her life. There could be no pleasure without having to "do without" first.

In early November all cakes and biscuits were banned. In fact it was like Lent only the weather was colder. The main thing was to "Think about other people" so even as a little girl I had to sit and make a present for everybody I knew. Most presents involved cutting out two disks from an old Weetabix packet and winding wool around them. I was famous throughout the neighbourhood for my pom-poms!

The slush and ice that greeted the New Year of 1952 was a different matter. People were cold and late for work but generally the feeling was that better things were coming.

THE FOURTH GENERATION

In early February the King died and was succeed by his daughter Elizabeth. We all looked forward to her Coronation. There was a war in Korea and that seemed very far away. At home people were delighted when tea rationing ended.

Cinema was the most popular form of entertainment as most people still not have a television. Charlie Chaplin came to Britain with his family for the premier of his film *Limelight* and was refused re-entry to the USA whilst he was being investigated.

Londoners had the West End where they could enjoy the theatre. *The Mousetrap* by Agatha Christie began its run at the Ambassadors. The New musical Express published the first up singles charts. Al Martinis "Here in my heart" was the first number 1.

Stylish women were wearing softer less structured clothes made out of crepe and chiffon. The single thing that appeared to worry most people was the "Cold War. It was called The Cold War because nobody actually did any fighting but we in the West were worried about being overtaken by the communists. England developed its own atomic bomb around this time. On the whole most people just enjoyed being alive without the fear of blackouts and shortages to spoil their daily routine.

It was late 1952 when Mona was asked by a neighbour if she wanted "an exchange" with her sister Beryl who lived in the new garden suburb.

Mona had been hoping for this and was highly delighted. However she would have to go on an eight mile journey to have a look at the house. The neighbour's sister's story was long on how lonely she felt without her family, but short on actual detail.

Mona was determined not to breathe a word of this to anyone. The fateful appointment day came and as she took off the apron she always wore, she pulled on her best herringbone swagger coat. She quickly dressed me in my best coat and shoes and she made a run for the bus stop before anybody could ask her what she was doing.

Unfortunately I was always travel sick, but she had come prepared and the forty five minute journey passed uneventfully. As we got nearer to our stop she could see a parade of shops, a church and a school.

THE FOURTH GENERATION

She stepped off the bus and looked around. Her first impressions were cool. She was not easily pleased but she could see that all the houses had lovely gardens and most important to her eyes everywhere looked clean and bright. She took the piece of paper with the number on out of her pocket. I was looking up expectantly and she said "I think we need no two hundred and eighty nine and after we have had a look we will walk to the shops and buy some chocolate".

As she walked around the green she began to realise that the number she wanted was a ground floor flat. This horrified her as she had been expecting a house. Her neighbour's sister opened the door to greet us with a big smile. My mother said frostily" I thought this was a house" as she stepped delicately over the threshold.

The sister winced and said "I thought you would not come if I told you but now you are here please look round" First impressions were favourable. There was a small kitchen with a cupboard and a cooker. A door, that only opened with a shove, led to a very well appointed wash house and outside to the garden. The garden backed on to fields and over the field stood a brand new primary school.

As we were ushered back inside we saw in this order a small hallway that could only be distempered, not painted because of damp, a living room that had a view of the Green, a tiny back hall, an immaculate separate bathroom and toilet and two bedrooms, one small and one medium.

As Mona pulled on her gloves and thanked her she said she would think about it. We walked hand in hand to the shopping parade and she told me she could not live in such a small space.

At the shopping parade was Hebert the Butcher, Hopkins the Grocer who delivered, the greengrocer, the cake shop and a paper shop that stocked the all-important *Manchester Guardian*. There was also a fish and chip shop that we would, of course, be having nothing to do with. As she waited for the bus she gave a big sigh, her dreams had been crushed.

CHAPTER 7
A New House means a New Baby

The next morning I was at nursery early as Mona had an appointment with the doctor. She had been feeling tired and under the weather. He examined her and asked a few pertinent questions before announcing" There's nothing wrong with you that will not be better in six months when this baby is born"

She burst into tears and for the life of her she did not know why as she would love a new baby. By the time she reached William's Brothers where she worked she had made a decision. She was going to take the flat. It was clean and bright, near a school and near two sets of shops. It would be a fresh start for her and Murray and she was sure that they would get a move to a house soon. I wonder if she had known that she would be there for fifteen years she would have made the same choices. They did buy a lovely house the year after my wedding and so her dream did come true eventually

When Murray arrived home that night he was asked to sit down as there were two pieces of news she had to share. The first was that he was going to be a father again in six months' time and the second was that they were moving to the garden suburb and the date of the move had been set for two weeks on Saturday.

He said later "I was elated at the first piece of news as I love babies but the second news filled me with dread. I was going to miss my pals and how on earth was I going to get to and from work as it was much farther away" When he asked her that question she fixed him with an icy stare and said "You will have to cycle, it will do you good"

The fateful Saturday arrived and Jack from next door knocked on the front door early. In common with most people we did not have many possessions and so it did not take long before we were on our way. When we arrived he helped us unpack and then he packed up the family who were going to live in our house.

My father never said a word. After he had been given a cup of tea and had a walk round the garden he declared himself satisfied and started to chat to George next door about soil conditions.

My first proper memory is of my Mother "running to the shops" to buy some groceries as it was snowing and I had the measles. I can remember clearly waiting at the window for her to return and the delicious taste and aroma of the tangerines she bought me as a treat.

My fourth birthday arrived and went without much celebration. I was vaguely disappointed as I been used to a lot of fuss. The combination of my mother's advancing pregnancy and the fact that we did not know the neighbours made it a quiet day. Mona was very disappointed that none of her siblings could come that day.

CHAPTER 8
Can I Look at her Please?

Psychologists tell us that our first real powerful memory is of our younger sibling's birth and for me that's true. My mother had been quite poorly and nearly lost the baby and so when I saw the man from next door helping my mother out of his car with the baby wrapped in a blanket I squealed with delighted. I went rushing out to meet them.

All I remember after that day is travelling on the bus backwards and forwards as we had to take the baby for treatment every single day. My mother was rhesus negative and my father was rhesus positive and my sister was one of the first babies to survive by transfusion. Once the baby was declared fit enough for three monthly visits to the hospital, my mother began to be a little less frosty with the neighbours.

Mrs Millicent who lived next door had kind eyes and a permanent smile. She had a lot to bear and I never saw her with a frown. Her daughter Susan who was the same age as me had been born with very severe cerebral palsy and needed constant care. Susan was in a wheelchair and could not do anything for herself. There was an older daughter Patricia who fascinated me .She had beautiful long hair and always wore full skirts with crinkly net underneath that swished as she walked.

The family next door to that were aptly named the Gardeners as they had the most beautiful garden in the area. Cedars of Lebanon trees grew forty feet ft. high in their garden and there was a constant battle with the council about whether they should be chopped down.

Mrs Biddy who lived next door to the Gardeners ruled the entire neighbourhood. She was the local busybody and keeper of the peace. She was the local school caretaker, who took in washing and looked after all aspects of her church.

The family were very devout Catholics and every room including the bedrooms had a statue of the Virgin Mary and a pot of Holy Water. At the back of the house there was a wash house where the activity never stopped. Mrs Biddy washed every day but Sunday. The activity involved boiling water which meant you could not see for all the steam. There was a posset to bash the clothes, a mangle to squeeze the water out, a washboard to get the collars clean and dolly blue to make the whites whiter.

I spent a lot of time in that wash house. Mrs Biddy had a daughter called Rosemary who was fourteen when we moved into the neighbourhood. She and her friend Delia were inseparable

About a week after we moved into the neighbourhood the two girls came to call and asked mother if they could take me for a walk. My mother agreed, she was glad of the help, and thus began an almost daily occurrence of them calling to take me out and about.

I remember a feeling of foreboding whenever they walked down the path but I had no choice but to go with them and I spent most of the time in their houses. My mother thought they were really helpful and because they looked after me so well, she could get on with lots of things.

It wasn't until many, many years later when I was at a Catholic wedding in Italy and I began to cry so hard that my husband had to take me out that I realised what that small child's feeling of foreboding had really been about.

Above us lived a man who had a breakdown when his wife left. She was much discussed in the neighboured because she wore her swimsuit in the garden when the weather was sunny. The general consensus of opinion was that he was better off without her.

Next door to us lived a frail old lady called Mrs Forest. She had had two sons. One son Dennis had died in the war and he was definitely her favourite. Pictures of him decorated every surface and every conversation sang his praises. The other son Norman still lived at home with her and although he had been engaged for many years she had forbidden him from getting married until she died. She did not care for his fiancée who appeared to my mother to be a charming lady.

Norman did everything for his mother and he was very kind to our family. He had bought his mother a puppy for company. This dog, Kim, was a Heinz 57 variety dog. The puppy had been given to them as part spaniel and part terrier. There was also part something else. This turned out to be Alsatian and the puppy just grew and grew until it was bigger than the old lady. She would not be parted with it and although the neighbourhood was in fear of it she controlled it with a wave of her hand.

Nancy who lived in the flat above her had two small children and kept to herself, but she turned out to an angel when my mother was very ill and I was left to look after the family.

Next door lived Ann and her three brothers. She became a real friend and her parents were charming and kind. I spent many happy hours playing in her garden

A shock of bright red hair tied with a scarf and a wonderful smile greeted anyone that knocked on Mrs Gannet's door. She lived with her two boys and two girls and an older man who she described as her father-in-law. Her husband had never been seen. She was shunned a little by the neighbourhood ladies "as she never, ever combed the children's hair"

There were two other things that happened in 1953 and they happened at the same time as my sister was born. We got a television and the Queen was crowned. We got the television to watch the coronation and as my sister was born on that day she was presented with a commemorative mug. With the new baby and all the excitement I never did see the Coronation. However a local paper described it thus.

"The Coronation of Queen Elizabeth second was a day of stunning pageantry that was celebrated around the world and marked the beginning of a long and historic reign."

CHAPTER 9
The Longest Day

My sister Gillian had been born the year before and she had demanded a lot of attention. She had a very pretty face with jet black hair and startling green almond shaped eyes. However she cried all the time with a very loud high pitched whine that set alarm bells off deep within my soul. I had been scared to even pass her pram for fear of starting her off again.

She had been one of the first rhesus babies ever to survive. My mother told me that "It's all those injections she had in her head to change her blood that have made her like this" As the following summer enveloped us in its warm embrace she started to walk and give me the most beaming smile as she pulled my hair as she passed me by.

The spectre of Hester who lived 8 miles away loomed large in our lives. My mother was always on edge when she was going to see her. Mona was tall and very slender and kept everything bottled up inside her. She would never tell you what she was feeling about anything at that stage of her life. She was private bordering on secretive. She hated what she called "neighbouring "and had been known to close the door whilst people were still talking.

Hester was small and round and her opinion on everything was available for everybody to hear very loudly all the time. She loved causing trouble and would give you what was euphemistically called "a clock" if you were passing by when she was in a rage.

Mona could not stand her and I loved her like life itself. It was a source of conflict between us over the years as my mother was convinced from the moment I was born that I was just like her mother.

Another sunny June day dawned and I was very excited about an imminent event. I was due to start school in September. I knew where the school was as it was also our church building for the time being. We were Methodists and we had no proper church and were saving up to have it built. The council had given us the land but the congregation had to find the money for the building.

THE FOURTH GENERATION

My mother had chosen the Methodists as she considered the high Church of England church that she had attended in her life "far too showy". This was another source of conflict with her mother. We lived in an area of Manchester where you knew everyone's religion as well as you knew their names. Catholics and Protestants lived side by side but attended different schools and churches. At our Methodist church we had a jolly vicar and a very glamorous deaconess .These two was very often in the neighbourhood in their normal clothes. The priest from the local Catholic Church was very tall and always dressed in the vestments of his office.

On a Friday night the priest could be seen accompanied by two tiny nuns in their flowing robes calling at each catholic house just as the father returned home. It was rumoured that it was to collect money for the new church roof but I never met anybody who confirmed that. I accompanied my mother to Thursday the housewife's group and we all went on a Sunday for a service and Sunday school.

I was a bright child who read avidly by the time I was 4 yrs. old so the thought of school held no fear. The only thing was I knew I could not run very fast or climb anything like the other kids. If a group of us were playing someone would shout "over the gate" and they would all disappear. I would be left looking at the gate thinking "How did they do that?"

It was to be a source of much rancour in my life as my lack of skill in that area included dancing, running, going down stairs and much more. I was the clumsy kid who made up for it by being helpful.

On that June morning we were due to go to Hester's for lunch. My mother was distant and distracted as I jumped about and squealed with excitement. She kept looking across at me as though she was making a decision. Finally she said "The baby has a poorly tummy and I am not taking her on the bus in that condition". My face fell as I had been looking forward to the outing." However" she continued, "you will be going as I cannot let my mother down as she is expecting us".

I was washed, dressed and out of the door before she could change her mind. She walked me across the green to the bus stop and as the bus pulled up she said to the conductor. "Here is her fare. She is to be put off outside the church on Princess Parkway."

The stop where I was getting off was on a very busy dual carriageway. To me she said "When you get off the bus wait at the side of the road until someone comes along to see you across" and with that she pushed me past the startled conductor and I sat down. As the engine started I looked back and saw her face as I disappeared into the distance. She looked very sad and I spent the whole journey worrying about her.

The first person to have an opinion that day was a lady who got on the bus two stops down. "Whatever is a child so young doing sitting on her own on a bus?" She and the conductor continued a long disapproving discussion until she got off the bus.

Finally after what seemed like hours the conductor shouted "This is you little girl, time to get off"

I gathered my belongings with as much confidence as I could muster and thanked him kindly for his assistance in this matter.

CHAPTER 10
I Can See St. Christopher's in the Distance

As the bus disappeared I stood at the side of the road. My confidence was beginning to desert me. I could see St Christopher's in the distance and I knew my Grandmother lived next door to the church. However I did not know how I could get past all these cars and buses that seemed, to a very small child, to be going very fast.

The dual carriageway had been built after the war. It was to carry the traffic to the suburbs that were being built at a breakneck speed and freight to the airport.

I remembered my mother's advice to wait for a kind stranger to see me across the road. I waited and waited as the cars flew past. There were some allotments not far away and eventually a man, who had been working in one of them, whilst occasionally peering over the fence to stare at me, came across to stand in front of me. He looked very cross and shouted "What are you doing here by a main road child?"

I explained that I needed to visit my Grandmother across the road. "Hold my hand" he said and grabbed me with the dirtiest hand I had ever seen. He was covered in soil and smelled of gardens but as he pushed his cap back I noticed his lined face looked very kind. He took me across the busy road, patted me on the back and disappeared again.

I stood for a moment to get my bearings and thought to myself "I have been told off twice this morning and I do not remember being naughty" I really had no idea what was to come.

I crossed a small road, went past a neighbour's house and skipped down my grandmother's path, my good spirits restored. Hester opened the door with a smile of greeting and looked straight ahead. She was dressed in her trademark V-necked top with pearls around the edge and a smart skirt. Her smart skirt reached her knees. Over it all she had a pinafore that she always wore to keep tidy. She had ditched her smart heeled shoes for flats a while back when she had a nasty fall on her way to work at the Opera House. She had twisted her knee and walking was difficult.

I looked up at her face. She still had curlers in her hair. She suffered from hair loss on top of her head, so she always stood erect. "All those babies took my hair with them," she used to say. She had no makeup on and so I studied the red veins on her cheeks whilst I waited.

I stared into the hall at the sweet peas on the piano that she had been trying to teach me to play. Most of her children were musical but my skill was limited to a tune called "Washing your Granddads shirt"

Finally she looked down and a terrible commotion broke out... She shrieked, her arms went up in the air whilst simultaneously trying to get her apron over her head and grab me at the same time. She shook me at the same time as trying to plant kisses on my face. She ran me into the kitchen whilst she was wailing at the irresponsibility of it all.

She shook so hard that the perpetual cigarette that she had at the corner of her mouth lost all its ash. Her face was very red and she burst into tears. She sat down on the stool by her kitchen range and summoned me to run next door to fetch Mrs Curtis who had the answer to everything.

As I ran through the vegetable patch I really had no idea what I had done wrong as I actually thought I had been a really good girl. Mrs Curtis ran back as fast as she could with me trying to keep up. She had not understood my description of my Grandma in distress and was convinced she was having a heart attack.

When we arrived back in the kitchen she realised Grandmother was not dead but just very upset. She turned to me and shouted "How dare you frighten an old lady like that I really thought Hester was dead you silly girl". She was probably fifty at the time.

She sat down on the other stool and I was instructed to fetch the cooking sherry whilst Mrs Curtis (I do not think she had a first name) and Grandma discussed the irresponsibility of her oldest daughter who had put the child on the bus.

After the second sherry Hester had calmed down enough to make a plan. She was to accompany me on the bus going back out into suburbs. The purpose of the journey was to give her daughter a piece of her mind. I knew this would not be good, but my mind was distracted by the delicious lunch that I had spied on the dining room table. Ham salad and the biggest piece of Cheshire cheese I had ever seen. Cheddar cheese was regarded as very common in our family and only to be used for cooking. There was also a gorgeous Victorian sponge which I never actually got to taste "It's a shame to spoil the look of it" was all she said.

I ate hastily whilst Mona went to the kitchen cupboard where she kept her pans. She took out her Ponds Cold cream and spread it liberally over her face. Then came the fascinating bit, she took out a box of powder and a large powder puff and applied it over the cream. As usual it went everywhere over her, over me and over all the kitchen work surfaces. She finished with the bright pink lipstick that she was never seen without, outside the house.

Mrs Curtis agreed to look after my youngest uncle when he came home from school. He was a pupil at William Hulme Grammar school and at eleven years old was considered old enough to travel on the bus and cross the dreaded road on his own. Sonny was blonde with green eyes and everybody said he was the handsomest boy they had ever seen. He was clever, charming and as the youngest child of all those children he was allowed to get away with anything .He had a very mischievous streak and was prone to running away. The word would go out that he had gone again and a posse of ladies in their aprons would fan out until he was spotted.

Sonny remained popular and charming all his life and over 1000 people attended his funeral when he died in his sixties. He never attained the glittering career that was expected of him but no-one could make you laugh like he could. He had the knack of making people feel better about them and spent his life helping other people.

When her friend agrees to stay and give her son his tea, Hester applied a liberal dose of perfume and we were off. Hester never really came to the suburbs on the bus. She preferred instead to go north to her job at the Opera House and for shopping trips.

I had a feeling of foreboding that kept me very quiet on the journey home. As we got nearer our stop Hester began to go redder and redder. We finally alighted and had to walk round the green as it had been raining and she did not want to spoil her good shoes. My mother had seen us through the window and was waiting at the front door which was round the side of the house. I tried to run to my bedroom to escape but Hester held me firmly in her clasp.

A huge shouting match ensued which consisted of Hester shouting and Mona staring at her. My mother was roundly told off for putting me on the bus on my own at five years old and as Hester got into her stride she was told off about everything her mother considered she was doing wrong.

The shouting was so loud that the lady whose front door faced ours, Mrs Millicent came running across to see if my mother needed help. She was swiftly followed by Mrs Biddy who had only come to see what was going on. Mrs Biddy was a caretaker at the local catholic school who was extremely nosy and clanked as she walked. The reason for the clanking noise was small milk bottles. Every school age child in the 1950s got a free third of a pint bottle of milk. This made for healthy children and kept the farmers busy. As a caretaker she brought the spare bottles home for the local kids. Nobody had a fridge then and so it had to be drunk straight away.

Years later Mrs Thatcher would become known as the "Milk Snatcher" when she stopped free school milk.

With that, Hester turned on her heel and marched off, never acknowledging the baby that was perched on my mother's hip. I knew the dark clouds were forming and that I was really in trouble. I didn't mind being shouted at or even slapped occasionally but I did mind upsetting my mother.

CHAPTER 11
These Rules Apply in our House

There were three cardinal rules in our little house:
   *One from Father.
   Never upset your mother or tell her your troubles as she is delicate.

   *One from Mother
 Never upset your father or behave cheekily as he works very hard and pays the bills.

   *One from them both.
Whatever happens never, never show us up in front of the neighbours or family.

I learned very early on to keep the peace and never tell your troubles. There was no peace to be kept that day. My mother was overcome with hurt about what her mother and her daughter had conspired to do to her. She cried and would not meet my gaze even though I tried to apologise over and over. She was very, very cross with me.

Eventually my father arrived home on his bike. He had got tired of cycling the eight miles to work and so had purchased a new-fangled engine fitted to the wheel. The idea was that if the engine did not work then you could still cycle home. The engine had stopped that morning yards from his factory so he had cycled all the way back.

He was not in a great mood when he came through the back door. I was summoned to be told off for my disgraceful behaviour. I could see tiny fragments of metal stuck to his rather roman nose as he bent down to tell me how disappointed he was in me. I had broken rule number one. I had upset my mother. This went on for some considerable time and I was beginning to feel rather faint as we had had no tea. Father announced he was far too upset to eat and needed a pint. He had a quick wash and was off to his local. By this time my mother had put the baby to bed and found her voice. Not only had I shamed her in front of that women (her mother) but I had broken rule no. two. I had upset my father. Worse than that my behaviour had caused him to go for a pint on a night that was not Friday and down that route lay ruin for us all. I was allowed a piece of Hovis with honey on before I went to bed.

As I was lying there trying to say my prayers I recollected that I had been scolded nine times that day. I thought it might be a world record. I was still only 5 yrs. Old and had been remonstrated with by The Lady on the Bus; the Bus Conductor; The Gardener; Grandmother; Mrs Curtis; My Mother; My Father and My Mother again. Finally I fell asleep with the church bells ringing ten pm.

CHAPTER 12
The Sound of Distant Relatives

It was the start of the summer holidays and the day dawned with the sun beaming through the thin pink curtains and an air of excitement and worry mixed together in my tummy. The night before I had lain awake for what felt like hours.

Mona said to me what she said every night "Close your eyes and say your prayers and God will send you to sleep" As my six year old eyes opened I saw my mother in her blue spotted overall over her second best dress and I tried to remember what I had been told.

"Your grandmother Alexandra is going on holiday and she is taking you with her" she sighed and added as an afterthought "you must remember to be a very good girl and do as you are told by the family.

I was dressed in my Sunday best yellow dress and navy Mary Jane shoes. My mother was a skilled dress maker and so made all mine and my two year old sister's clothes. I was given a shopping bag which contained two other dresses, a nightdress and underwear and a pair of slippers.

"Make sure you eat your breakfast and here is a sandwich for your journey," my mother said, and then shooed me out of the house and across the green to the bus stop.

There was nobody waiting so as the bus stopped my mother stepped forward and said to the conductor "She is going all the way to Manchester and will be met at the terminus by her grandmother". As I turned to say goodbye I noticed she had a very sad face and I spent the whole ten mile journey worrying about her. I had been on the bus on my own before to deliver messages or meet people but I felt very grown up and chatted to passengers who spoke to me.

As we pulled into Piccadilly I saw Alexandra and Hubert waving at me from the side of the road. I gathered my green gabardine coat and my bag and ran towards them.

My Father's mother was a jolly sort who did not obey 1950s dress code. She looked very jaunty in her brightly coloured outfit and wonderful hat. "We are going to have to run as our coach leaves in about fifteen minutes" she shouted as she pulled me along with her husband struggling to keep up. He had been gassed in the First World War and had problems keeping up.

As we boarded the coach I was filled with excitement and was herded into the window seat. The journey was punctuated by boiled sweets, egg and tomato sandwiches and regular stops. I was so bored, hour after hour and as dusk turned to darkness we arrived at Norwich bus station.

I turned to my grandmother who was a little less jaunty after sitting on a cramped coach for 12 hours and asked "Where are we going now?" Her face was full of concern "Well Granddad and I are going on that coach over there but you are staying here".

I looked around at the cold, grey building with the smell of diesel in the air and the darkness descending. "Your Great Uncle Arthur was due to meet us here but I cannot see him anywhere. It would help if I knew what he looked like but I cannot wait around as Granddad Hubert will be cross if we miss our connection."

I was marched to the nearest man in a uniform where she explained I was on my way to family in Great Yarmouth and someone was due to collect me. With that she turned on her tail and disappeared into the night. The man in the uniform took pity on me as he said he had daughters of his own and would wait with me.

We waited and we waited and we waited. Eventually a rather jolly chap with a large moustache and a trilby turned up. He was very breathless and bent down to take my hand. I had absolutely no idea who he was, "I am Uncle Arthur, son of your Great Grandmother Hannah and half-brother of your Grandmother Hester and I am pleased to make your acquaintance"

The man in the uniform waved goodbye and we hurried along to a very large car parked at the front of the bus station. "Climb in the back dear and try not to go to sleep because Great Grandmother Hannah is waiting up for you, especially"

I only remember the claustrophobic smell of new leather and air freshener and I was fast asleep. I awoke to see the tinniest person I had ever met. At 4ft 10ins with silver hair down to her waist she looked like something out of a fairy tale. The thing that was most striking about her though were her bright green almond shaped eyes and quiet tinkling voice

"Come with me, darling and welcome to my tiny house. We have met before but you were only small and I am sure you will not remember me" She had run hotels all her life but retired to a tiny, terraced house near her children.

The first thing I noticed as I crossed the threshold was a large apricot poodle that growled rather alarmingly and I was sure we were never going to be friends. I just had time to ask for a glass of milk before I fell into a deep sleep on a lovely, squishy feather bed

CHAPTER 13
I get Breakfast in Bed?

The next day dawned sunny and bright and for a few moments I had no idea where I was. Then Hannah popped her head round the door to ask if I would like breakfast in bed.

I had no idea what she was talking about, who ate their breakfast in bed? No-one in my house that was for sure!. She returned moments later with a tray with a cloth and the most exquisite china and silverware. There was a lovely boiled egg, toast and jam and a glass of something that tasted of sweet oranges.

Hannah was dressed in a brown gabardine suit with a high necked white blouse with a frilled collar at her neck she wore a beautiful cameo and in each ear was a pink pearl. Her silver hair was neatly plaited and wound around and around her head. I discovered that was the way she dressed every day, rain or shine. She smelled of violets and would not have dreamed of leaving home without lipstick, earrings and perfume. This was a legacy from her hotel owning days.

She said "I will leave you to get dressed and see you by the front door in about fifteen minutes as we are going for a walk". She looked through my bag of clothes and nodded, she seemed to find them satisfactory.

I stared around me in wonder. A tiny window had white curtains with snow drops on them and the eiderdown matched. There was a little white wardrobe and chest of drawers with a china pitcher in a bowl. I put my feet on the floor and there was a lovely soft rug. I thought I might get to like this.

By the time I was six I was quite a large child with jet black hair cut very short and straight.

I had very rosy cheeks and both my front teeth were missing. Cleanliness was next to Godliness in my house so everything had to be scrubbed before dressing for the day. I had two large clips to hold my hair in place. I dreamed of long hair like the other girls. My Mother insisted on short hair as it was easier to manage. She herself had long hair held in place in a bun and so I failed to see her logic.

Once I was dressed I made my bed and put my few clothes away. I crept down the tiny staircase to be faced by the mean dog and a singing canary.

As I wondered how to get passed these formidable opponents Hannah arrived with a hat and stout shoes. Every day of her life she breakfasted on sweet tea with a dash of brandy. This put colour in her cheeks and a mischievous glint in her eye.

"We are off to the beach and I am going to tell you about all the family. You are going to meet them all and it would be good if you knew a little bit about them"

As a little girl the concepts of rich or poor never crossed my mind. I knew my Dad worked in a factory. I knew we had to tighten our belts because along with lots of other men my dad was on "short-time". This was a phrase I used a lot which caused the family to collapse into fits of laughter.

CHAPTER 14
Cook Your Vegetables very Well

My mother budgeted very carefully. She shopped every day and you would never, ever take food or a drink without asking permission. Like many other families in the 1950s we had the same food on each day of the week. Plain food with the vegetables cooked for at least an hour. We had a roast on Sunday which had been cooked the day before and allowed to go cold. This meant it could be sliced very thinly and goes much further.

On Monday the roast was chopped and covered with mashed potato, shepherd's pie;

Tuesday was liver and onions;

Wednesday was egg and chips;

Thursday was Lancashire hot pot made with half a pound of stew meat;

Friday was fish; everybody ate fish on a Friday;

Saturday was Mother's day off from cooking and we had sandwiches or salad depending whether we had company.

It dawned on me on that first day talking to my tiny great grandmother that life in East Anglia was very different to Manchester. As we sat on the beach eating ice-cream she told me all about her five children who lived close by. She spoke to me gently about all her children including my Grandmother Hester who I loved dearly. She must have explained in words a little girl could understand but only the names remain in my mind.

Her favourite was her youngest Michael. He was in his early twenties then and much younger than her other children. He was recently married to Anna and I only met him once on that visit. Her oldest son Arthur had been born just a year after she had run away from Manchester followed closely by David, Dorothy and Violet.

I was to meet them all in the following few days but by then we were ready for lunch. My first impression of lunch was being taken up some steps into a beautiful room. The room was full of tables with starched, white cloths, shining silver and vases of flowers. A smartly dressed waiter rushed over to greet Hannah and ruffle my hair.

The table was set for three and joining us was a very severe lady who looked me up and down and said "OH, so this is the child." She never spoke another word to me during my whole visit. This was my great aunt Dorothy who owned this restaurant and the attached hotel. She was not fond of my Grandmother, her half-sister and the cause of the rift between them was shrouded in mystery. The lunch was brown Windsor soup, followed by fish and then trifle. I ate every morsel, said "Thank you" and never saw her again.

The following day was much more fun. As we took a stroll along the promenade Hannah turned left, walked a little way and then knocked on a huge green door. As the door opened the smell and taste of sugar filled my senses.

A large, jolly man in a white coat and hat came forward to greet us and said "Hello young lady, my name is Cyril and I will be showing you round today "There was so much noise with machinery clanging and women chattering cheerfully doing what was mostly a manual job.

Seaside rock was a popular sweet treat in the 1950s and was made by mixing granulated sugar and glucose syrup together. It was boiled in vats and then rolled by hand. The letters inside were made by combining thin strips of different coloured and white rock.

The colour pink and the smell of peppermint filled the space for miles and miles. This was the biggest rock factory in the area and owned by Hannah's daughter Violet and her husband Cedric. As the tour came to a close I was presented with a box containing enough rock for all my family.

Violet and Cedric had a beautiful house on the cliff edge and I was to be taken there that afternoon. We walked back to Hannah's house for lunch with the sounds of the seagulls and the smell of the sea assailing my senses.

THE FOURTH GENERATION

A Rolls Royce came to collect us at 2pm sharp. A chauffeur assisted Hannah into its spacious interior and he carefully lifted me in. The drive did not take long but I was transported to another world. The gates opened slowly and through the trees I could see a magnificent house. As we stopped they came down the steps to greet us. I loved Violet from the moment I saw her. She was glamorous with blonde hair swept into a chignon and so beautifully dressed but the best thing was she looked just like my mother. She was carrying a little white dog that she called "Baby".

Cedric was very smartly dressed with jet black hair and a narrow moustache. He spoke with an American accent and smelled of cologne when he picked me up and swung me round and around. The house was amazing with every modern appliance 1950s Britain could offer. There was a huge television screen on the wall, carpets that you sunk to your knees in and flowers everywhere.

A bell was rung and a maid brought us afternoon tea and then the car was summoned and Hannah, Violet and I went shopping. The dress was chosen for me Navy with a sailor collar.

I was allowed to choose a bracelet. I was offered a choice of a shiny Marquisette bracelet or a solid silver one with charms that was not at all shiny. I loved the shiny bracelet and Violet said to me "The other one is worth many times more and you will be able to add to it but it's your choice. I of course loved the marquisette and it was duly wrapped and presented to me. I remembered my manners and expressed my thanks. She rewarded me with a kiss on the cheek and promised to see me the next day.

In the car I asked Hannah if they had any children and she whispered "shuhhh"... it's very sad.

CHAPTER 15
Kippers for Tea?

That evening we walked along the sea front and botanical gardens. The fairy lights were magical to my child's eyes and I was beginning to imagine that I could live in this fairy land forever, especially when we stopped for fish and chips on the way home.

The next morning there was a knock on the door and there was Cedric who had come to take me on a trip. He owned lots of businesses and one factory was for the world renowned "Suttons Kipper Fillets." We had to put on white coats and hats before we stepped into the smokehouse.

Kippers are herrings that have been caught, butterflied and then cold smoked over smouldering woodchips. The men that worked in there were impervious to the smell and smoke but my little lungs could not take it and I emerged coughing and spluttering.

Kippers were very popular then and I was about to have my first and last taste. We settled for lunch in the restaurant where I had kippers, bread and butter, a glass of fizzy pop and a knicker bocker glory. I felt extremely bilious in the Rolls Royce back home and I have never eaten knicker bocker glories since. (Or kippers for that matter!)

The week settled into a lovely routine and I met Hannah's other sons. Arthur, who had collected me, had been the man of the family since his father died and took care of all the family business. He had another hotel further along the sea front and had a son and a daughter both of whom lived in London.

David and his wife Gloria lived in their hotel further along the coast. They invited me for tea and we all crammed into a small sitting room where the whole family including two children lived and slept. I could not understand how they could live in one room when they had a big hotel. The answer of course was that the paying customer was king.

On the Thursday night a family party was held in my honour where I amused everyone by saying that I thought the food tasted better in the North.

THE FOURTH GENERATION

On Friday night Hannah ran me a bath of two inches of water "in case I drowned" and said how much she would miss me. I was very confused and said "I am actually here for a fortnight, didn't you know?"

Hannah was very perplexed and had to sit down on the cork stool. She was sure I was going home the next day. What to do? There were no phones any way of getting in touch. She eventually went to get the letter that my mother had sent months before arranging the trip. She read and re read it but finally it was clear. Alexandra and Hubert would be in Norwich a week on Saturday and I was to meet them at eleven o'clock sharp as the coach back up North was leaving an hour later.

Well the visit went decidedly downhill from there on. She was still kind to me and fed me but she had a life to get on with. Although she sold her own hotel she still worked for all her children in differing capacities

That week I had a crash course in hotel management. I polished silver, acres of silver. I made sandwiches and sat quietly in corners watching what was going on. I helped change beds and chatted to anyone that would listen. I was also left alone a lot in the little house with the canary and the poodle.

My mother hated flies and so along with every family in the land she had a plastic bottle of DDT on the window ledge. When flies started circling the lightshade in great grandma's sitting room I knew just what to do. I stood on the stool, reached the window ledge and began to squirt DDT to my heart's content.

When Hannah arrived home she found a coughing little girl with her eyes streaming, a partially expired poodle who was never the same again and a completely expired canary whose singing days were behind him. When all the hysterics died down and the doctor dispatched I was told never to mention the incident to my mother.

Finally Saturday came and Arthur drove me to meet Alexandra and Hubert at the bus station. They were tanned and relaxed and had lots of stories to tell about a lovely holiday. The journey felt interminable and I was fast asleep when my Father met me at the bus stop.

My mother said "We will talk about it tomorrow" to my many questions. It was years later I discovered that Michael was in fact Hester and Frank's son and had gone for a holiday age three years and was never returned. He called his Grandmother "Mama" and took her surname.

The baby that Violet and Cedric had lost was also Hester's son that she had born to help her childless sister. He died when he was nine months old of scarlet fever.

The rift between Hester and Dorothy was because Dorothy had discovered that Hannah was still in fact married to William and not to her father. She was scared that the volatile Hester would spill the beans.

So that was my trip to see the relatives and there is not much to say except that if anyone has a vacancy at a hotel, a rock factory or a kipper smoking shed, I can fill in at a moment's notice!

CHAPTER 16
Watching Father's Teacakes

I loved school and from the very first day looked forward to going. It was an ordinary school led by an extraordinary woman: the formidable Miss Johnson. The story was that she had lost her fiancé in the war. She believed absolutely in streaming and always said after she had walked around the new infant intake she could tell you who was going to grammar school. From being small we were tested and then sat at the table that was based upon our score. Each class had approximately 36 children in it.

The baby boom years had arrived and six tables of six were dotted around the classroom. Your heart sang when you moved to the top table and your face was red with shame if you got moved down one.

I loved infant school. It was easy and we had a gentle teacher who took care of us. By the time we started junior school at 6 or 7 we could all tell our times table as it had been drilled into us. We recited it every morning and every afternoon before we left. I found that I had a real problem when I went up to junior school.

THE FOURTH GENERATION

The new classroom was on the first floor. We all had to assemble with our given partners and hold hands. Miss Bruney, who was rather a severe red head, shouted "Forward" and we were all meant to run down the stairs in order.

The first day was a disaster. I was near the front and I already had evidence that my feet and brain were not attached. "Still" I thought "what harm can I do" but little did I know?

As I started to run forward my feet went from under me and I fell down and the poor hapless boy I was holding hands with did too. Every pair of children that followed us, landed on the children in front and it was carnage. There were tears and moans and teachers came running from all directions.

I was hoping to get away with it but Geoffrey who I was holding hands with shouted "It was her Miss." I am afraid Geoffrey had an axe to grind with any girl in his class. His mother brought him to school every day and picked him up in the afternoon. In the 1950s nobody's mother did that and he was the odd one out. She compounded his shame by putting a clip in his hair to keep it out of his eyes and some of the mean girls giggled.

In those days if you fell over the school dealt with it and never dreamt of telling your parents. It is different today thank goodness. The children get a sticker for any minor mishap and parents are summoned if there is anything more major.

The thing I remember most from that morning was the smell of iodine which had been liberally doused on any injury. That and the many teachers who tried to teach me to run downstairs. Eventually Miss Johnson was called and she bent down and said in a posh but kind voice "Come on dear, I will show you how, it's not that difficult." She did very well until she had to round the bend on the stairs, missed her footing and fell to the bottom in a dishevelled state. I was sure that posh but kind voice shouted "Oh, Christ!" as she fell but my mother said I must have been imagining it.

After the ambulance had left with Miss Johnson safely inside, as she had badly sprained her ankle the teachers got together and decided I could walk downstairs after the other children had arrived safely.

My mother was great at letting me use the oven. She did not have a lot of interest in cooking as she preferred sewing. Hester was teaching me to cook something different every time I saw her.

I learned how to make sauces, stews, bake bread and pies and fancy deserts, which I tried out on the family. The only thing my mother insisted on supervising was the gravy. Two large tablespoons of Bistro mixed with a little water. Add a pan full of cold water and stir on a low light for twenty minutes.

We called it gravy punishment in our house because your arm would be dead and your fingers burned by the time you finished. It was also critical to lay the table half an hour before sitting down to eat.

I made friends with a girl called Veronica and stayed for tea at her house. I reported to my mother that Veronica's mother did not lay the table and made her gravy with the boiling water that the carrots had been in. Mona glared at me and said "Some women have no idea"

There were two other horrible jobs that seemed to fall to me. One was "Watching father's teacakes." This involved bending down and staring hypnotically at the waist high grill to be sure his morning teacakes did not catch. I concentrated, I really did but the teacakes always got burnt and occasionally caught fire. This involved much carry on and poor father had to take Ryvita with jam on to work for his morning snack.

The other job was "drying the dreaded plastic bags". We only had four as they were new-fangled and had to be washed and dried within an inch of their lives. I hate plastic bags to this day.

Mother also insisted on washing the dishes the absolute second the last person finished their meal. To leave them was regarded as slovenly and would not be tolerated at any price.

CHAPTER 17
The Lady Mayoress

I was using my baking skills to make cakes to sell to make money for the new church. I took them round all the neighbours. My skills in that direction were noted and everyone was very pleased when the Methodist church was finally built. The big question was who would present the bouquet to the Lady Mayoress. The answer turned out to be little old helpful me and my mother made me a wonderful outfit. I had a straw boater with a ribbon and my photograph in the *Manchester Evening News*.

I sometimes wonder if that was the pinnacle of my success. I did not fare so well in the Brownies. I was a child that was always cheery but occasionally would blurt out what I was thinking when sometimes it would be better left unsaid. This went down very badly with the rather severe lady that ran the Brownies.
The real problem was that I couldn't skip. To pass my first set of badges I had to recite the motto "I promise to do my best for god and the Queen and help other people every day, especially those at home." I could do that with my eyes closed.

Make a rice pudding.(Easy Peasy.)

Make a garden in a dish.(I loved planting bulbs.)

Help at home.(I did that anyway.)

The thing that held me back was that skipping.

The Grandmothers were summoned to show me how to skip as my mother had one of her many twisted ankles and couldn't do it. Mona never left home without an emergency crepe bandage as a twisted ankle could strike her anytime. Coming out of the Co-op, on the cobbles in Edinburgh, pushing the pram, even washing up one day when she was on a completely flat surface.

She did not care what country she was in either. She needed that emergency crepe bandage camping in Canada, on a fishing boat in Cuba and running up some steps in St Petersburg, She also carried emergency Thermagene in case she had a bad back and Dr Potter's cold pills in case she was feeling under the weather.

Thermagene was furry and bright red and you put it next to your skin to help a bad back. When I was suffering one day I asked for a little piece that was duly granted. It was tucked into my navy knickers with the pocket and pushed up the back of my liberty bodice. I forgot ten minutes later and went for a wee with disastrous consequences. The red furry material fell into the lavatory, frightening the life out of me, causing me to scream. My mother came running and realising I was ok proceeded to be very cross as I had wasted the Thermogene that "cost a lot of money "I was relegated to being smothered in Deep Heat when I had an ache or strain.

My grandmothers Hester, Alexandra and a gaggle of neighbourhood children were all standing in a line by the coal house door on a little patch of lawn. This was the only useful bit of grass as father had taken up the rest with growing beautiful flowers gladioli, dahlias and sweet peas were his favourites. He also grew lettuce for the rabbit who stared at us with disdain. He was a very snooty rabbit and I do not know where he got his airs and graces from.

The grandmothers who very rarely met but tolerated each other had known each other since childhood. Hester small and plump but with tiny feet and hands started skipping first. She was made for skipping because she had a low centre of gravity. She stopped quite quickly as she was out of puff, the Senior Service she smoked had taken its hold. Alexandra went next, taller and more agile I could hear her bracelets tinkling as she went up and down.

"Easy" they both cried in unison, that old thing again. My feet and brain were not attached, I couldn't do it. After many attempts I was allowed back in the house. The family conference decided that my father would take me to Brownies on Monday night to ask for special dispensation. He was very handsome and could get away with anything with his twinkling eyes.

Monday night came around and I felt really proud as he accompanied me into the church hall. He made his request and was met with a deathly silence by Brown Owl.

"I know, I know" shouted Tawny Owl who had been listening to the conversation from behind the cupboard "She can make two rice puddings instead of skipping" and so everybody saved face. I remain to this day the only Brownie who was ever allowed to make a rice pudding in order to receive her skipping badge.

There was a definite dark cloud looming over the extended family at the end of 1957.

CHAPTER 18
The Sisters have left the Country

My aunt Amy was the cleverest of all the children. She also was a talented musician and loved life. She had won a scholarship to Manchester High School for girls and got 9 high grade O levels, which was an achievement in those days. The school were desperate for her to stay on and do her levels and try for Cambridge University.

A meeting was called and Hester went along. When the Headmistress explained the position she announced. "This will not happen; she has to go to work" and she added as an afterthought "If anybody goes it will be my youngest son"

With a heavy heart Amy found a job in banking and proceeded to fly up the ranks. However she was still unhappy about being denied University that when a friend suggested going to Vancouver she agreed. They both got transfers with the Bank.

My aunt Jane worked in fashion and had just got married. She got carried away with all the excitement and soon both her and her new husband Jack had got jobs in Vancouver too.

Aunt Beth who was 25 had been married for a couple of years owned a lovely house. She was a secretary at the Manchester Evening News. Her husband Eric had family in Vancouver. His brother had moved out years before and ran the Vancouver Football Team. Beth got tenants for her house and secured a job at the Vancouver Star and announced to everyone that she and Eric would be leaving with the other girls. That left my mother as the only daughter left in England as well as all the brothers.

Hester sank into a deep depression .She was 52 yrs. old and for the first time in her life had lost absolute control over her children. My mother felt she had been left to pick up the pieces and she too became completely overwhelmed by her sister's disappearing from her life.

In 1957 many young British people were heading for Canada. In the proceeding 3 years 150,000 Britons had left to make a new life there. The adventurous traveller chose the speed and glamour of the aeroplane. The problem was the 6000 miles flight to Vancouver took twenty seven hours with two stopovers.

Some British men had left their wives and children at home to try and make their fortune. A neighbour's husband went to Alberta to work in the mines. She coped with 5 children on her own and without her mother and sister's generosity she would have not survived. She had not one dollar from him in the two years he was away. She told me "I heard him whistling in the kitchen, **I** could not believe he was home. His first words were can you nip out and pay the taxi, love".

Another friend Ken went by boat from Liverpool to Montreal. He worked his way across Canada to British Columbia where he found a job in the lumber industry. He experienced freezing cold winters and the mosquito invaded summers but this did not detract from the enjoyment of his life. He was a lumbar jack and he was alright!

A big family party was waiting for our weary aunts and uncles when they arrived. Beth's husband's aunt had been one of the first women to emigrate to British Columbia. She had had a big family there so there were lots of cousins to welcome them to The Sunshine Coast.

Amy looked across the room at distant cousin John, who was an engineering student and that was that. Love at first site they married and came to England on a year's study scholarship at Manchester University. They returned to Vancouver to live and raise their family. Beth enjoyed her job at the newspaper but could not settle and came back two years later to live in England.

Jane got a job in the burgeoning film industry and she and her husband came back a few times to England to live but eventually settled on Vancouver Island.

However my mother did not know at this time whether she would ever see her sisters again and Christmas that year was very subdued. We all gathered at Hester' house for the Christmas day party but nobody's heart was in it. Even the dog Lassie looked unhappy. As we stood at the bus stop waiting for the bus to take us home from Grandmother's house I looked at my mother and really wished I could cheer her up.

CHAPTER 19.
My Year of Good Works

I was becoming more religious and saying prayers in the morning as well as in the evening. As the New Year dawned I made a pact with myself to help more people. I think I envisaged being more helpful emotionally and spiritually but it turned out to actually involve quite a lot more physical work.

I looked around to see who would benefit from my help. Well my sister obviously. She came most places with me. Although we were 4 years apart **we** were always dressed like twins. We looked completely different to all the other kids as we were so neat and tidy.

She was highly emotional and prone to bouts of tears. You could be guaranteed to make her cry by showing her the parents' wedding photo. The same thing happened every time.
 She would say with rising alarm "But where was I?"
I would say with rising glee "You were not even born"
And she would go completely hysterical and cry so hard her forehead would go very red. Our mother would fly in and gently take the photo from her little hand. I knew that made me a mean girl but a very good older sister in every other way!
I made a list in my diary of all my skills
    *Definite known skills.
    *Saying my prayers.
    *Doing most housework.
    *Doing a lot of gardening.
    *Reading to small children.
    *Writing letters for old ladies.
    *Cooking and baking.
    _*Cutting hair.
    *Taking dogs for a walk. (Only small ones)
    *No skill at all and not likely to develop one.
    *Jumping.
    *Running.
    *Dancing.
    *Singing.
    *Balancing on a tightrope.(never tried but not likely)

THE FOURTH GENERATION

*Painting.

I knew I did not want to do anybody's ironing or travel far on a bus. I looked at this list for a long time and then weighed up the known facts. I knew I could not dance as I had been to Mrs Jones ballet class for three weeks the year before. When my Mother attended the show I was in, she was silent all the way home. When I asked her what she thought she said "Well let's just say we won't be wasting two shillings a week on that again." Ballet was never mentioned in our house again. I knew I could not sing as Mr Alsop the school music teacher had shouted, "Be quiet girl" while the choir was practising.

I knew I could not paint as when Mrs Mills my teacher looked at my painting of a boat she had gone to get Mrs Clegg to look at it. I secretly hoped they were going to complement me

They both stood over me and Mrs Clegg let out a huge snort. She laughed that much that her asthma was set off and somebody had to run to fetch her inhaler. I had known from early on that I could not run, jump or balance so I had ruled tightrope walking out with trying it.

I sat on my bed and decided I was not going to feel too disappointed as I was not sure how these things could help anyone.
My help people list eventually contained
>*Reading
>*Writing letters
>*Shopping
>*Cooking
>*Baking
>*Gardening.
>*Cutting Hair

I had ruled out dog walking as I remembered that I had been bitten the year before when I was running down the hill. I had fallen and my dress was covered in mud. There had been such a commotion about the mud that I did not dare mention my bitten leg until I was about to get into bed.

Hot water was precious so you were only allowed a bath during the week in emergency. This must have constituted one as I was soon up to my neck in steam and a liberal helping of Dettol. My father was dispatched to Clifford's house, as the offending dog was his, to give his mother a piece of my mother's mind.

My first helpful act was to write down the football scores for my father as he was working overtime. I sat down in front of the television and wrote down every number that was shouted out by the man with a nice voice. When he said, "Arsenal 2 Manchester United 4 I wrote down 2 and 4 because I could not remember the team's names. I filled several pages of Basildon Bond note paper with these numbers and although I knew I was taking a risk that I would be in trouble for wasting paper I thought he would be very happy. He stared and looked very perplexed by the rows of single numbers and then continued to stare. I could not believe he was so unappreciative of my endeavours and I burst into tears.

My second helpful act was to take a plank out of the shed and try to straighten the edges of his lawn with the spade. I went around and around as I could not really get a straight line anywhere. It took absolutely ages. When he arrived home he was greeted with a postage stamp size lawn with crooked edges. I had also stood on every daffodil that was just raising its head. My father took one look and he burst into tears.

My last helpful act was to take my sister to the ironmongers to buy mother a new pan. I had noticed that the pan she boiled the eggs in was too big and so thought she would be pleased with a smaller one. The pan was not a success and was duly returned. Mother asked me to stick to flowers if I wanted to buy presents again. I thought I might cry but just shrugged my shoulders and decided to give up being helpful.

She came to me a few weeks after the incident of the pan and said "If you are feeling helpful there is something you can do to help me. I really want to buy a fridge and have a holiday this year so it would be very helpful if you could look after your sister in the morning whilst I am at work." By that time my sister had started school and mother's working hours would be during school time. I was needed to look after her in the holidays. I was 8yrs and Gillian was 4yrs old.

The first day really set the pattern for the rest of the school holidays. I would get up and get dressed as soon as mother went out and make breakfast. I had plans to read to my sister and complete some of the tasks on my list. I would ask Gillian to get up and she would refuse. Each morning she stayed in bed until 5 minutes before mother was due home and then we stood at the window smiling and waiting for her to come round the corner.

CHAPTER 20
The Fringe that went Up and Down

The only incident of note in that time was when I attempted to give her a haircut before she went on her holidays. Cutting hair was something I really wanted to try as it looked easy with fast results. I started with her fringe and then went round in a circle. Whatever I did it looked worse and by the time mother came home it was beyond dreadful. If my sister had sat still it would have helped All mother said was "It's a good job we are going on holiday on Saturday. The fridge is paid for and I hated that job anyway"

The day of the holiday to Clevelys duly arrived and we piled in the hire car. We were staying at a bed and breakfast run by the most miserable woman you would ever meet. She had a huge bosom and a very imperious manner.

The list of what you could and could not do was very long and included leaving the minute breakfast was over and not returning until 6pm for dinner. It rained and rained that week and was freezing cold. We just walked about shivering in our summer clothes. Mother declared she would never go on holiday again as it was such a waste of money and I think we all were inclined to agree with her.

We got the new fridge and ITV when we got back. I do not know what pleased me more. Having ice cold milk on my Frosties or having a choice of television programmes. Blue Peter started that year which we loved. The two things in the news I overheard my parents discussing were the Cod war with Iceland and that Bertrand Russell had founded CND.

The great personal news was that Aunt Amy had come back from Canada with her new husband. She was lovely and determined to improve our lives culturally. She arranged a trip to see The

Nutcracker Suite Ballet in Manchester and said she would meet us at the bus stop near Grandma's house.

We were duly dressed in our finery and put on the bus to meet them at four pm which left time to have tea before the performance. As I was getting older it was assumed that I knew where I was going and the bus conductor was not told where we needed to get off.   Of course it goes without saying that we got off the bus four stops too soon, caused a big panic about where we were and not only missed tea but missed the ballet as well.

There is one more bus story to tell that happened just before Christmas.

CHAPTER 21
Two Three foot Dolls

My grandmother Alexandra lived on the other side of Manchester and we needed to take two buses. You had to take one into the city and one out again to her house. She was very generous at Christmas and loved to treat us. She really did not cook much and just made salad which you had to check carefully for caterpillars.

As the ladies headed out to go shopping the men sat down for a chat about the war and football. As we left we noticed that Hubert produced a bottle of thick purple liquid.

We had a lovely afternoon and went to a little shop where Grandmother had ordered each a felt ice-skating skirt with bobbles on and a matching pair of shoes. Mine were red and Gillian's were green. When we arrived back at the house it was time to go and as we said our goodbyes she presented us with a beautiful doll each. The only problem was that each was in a box about three feet long.

Our father with a big beaming grin on his face insisted that he could carry a box on each shoulder. We had a half mile walk to the bus stop to get into central Manchester. It was not long before mother realised that the combination of a small salad, fresh air and a whole bottle of whatever the purple liquid was has rendered father incapable of carrying himself never mind to very large dolls in boxes. With a large sigh she took a child in each hand and walked on ahead to the bus stop leaving him to catch up.

We managed the journey into Manchester but as we crossed Piccadilly it was obvious we were in trouble. Father wove this way and that always managing to keep a doll on his shoulder.

We boarded the bus for home and knew it was going to be a long eight miles. My Mother sat me on the outside of father and implored me to keep him in his seat. She sat down on the opposite side of the bus with my sister on her knee and pretended she did not know us. I sang to him and I chatted to him but four miles from home he decided he needed to get off the bus as he felt so ill.

I moved swiftly aside and he walked to the back of the bus and he must have seen two rails that night as he chose the wrong one and stepped off the bus into the night.

No one said a word. My mother carried on taking to us as though nothing had happened. The conductor shrugged his shoulders. The other passengers were shocked into silence. I felt so worried I had a pain in my middle.

When we reached our stop my mother gathered her children, her shopping and the two biggest dolls she had ever seen and got off the bus. She walked home put her children to bed and contemplated life as a widow.

She was fast asleep when she heard knocking on the door. When she looked at the clock it was three am. She assumed it was the police coming to tell her of his demise and so straightened her hair and put her dressing gown on. When she opened the door she was delighted and furious in equal measures. There he stood battered, bruised and bloodied from his fall and missing his false teeth. He was also stone cold sober from his four mile walk in the fresh air.

Two things happened after that fiasco. The very next week he bought a car, as my mother was determined she would never get on a bus again. He also determined never again to drink mulberry wine offered by veterans of the First World War.

CHAPTER 22
Cheddar is for Cooking Purposes Only

Christmas was wonderful that year. Hester was in good form as one of her daughters was home from Canada with her new Canadian husband, John. He spoke with a slow drawl. Hester liked him because he had good manners but she remarked "He takes so long thinking about his answer to any question that by the time he answers I have forgotten what I was talking about"

My sister Gillian and I thought he was amazing because he could put a whole chocolate teacake in his mouth at once. That would just not be allowed in our house.

That Christmas had been lots of fun. Sonny had learned to play the guitar and with his blonde hair looked just like a pop star. His friend Graham could play the washboard and that just added to the general air of happiness. Sonny and Graham had a small repertoire limited to the Everley brothers and Buddy Holly songs. We did not care as they were our favourites.

We all shouted encore after renditions of Peggy Sue, That'll be the day, Walk Right Back and Crying in the Rain.

I remember laughing so hard when one of the uncles got bored with the noise and after asking politely for it to stop got up and placed an orange in Sonny's mouth. That really shut him up! I stood with my sister in my Grandmother's dining room surveying the marvellous Christmas tea table.

Hester regarded as a personal insult if anyone left her table hungry and so provided copious amounts of food. From the left there was the largest ham we had ever seen, glistening and smelling delicious. I did not care for the cloves on top as they made your mouth tingle if you accidently bit into one. However it was worth the pain to taste the sweet honey coating underneath.

There were two huge pieces of cheese, one was Cheshire (suitable) and one was Cheddar (not sure if this was allowed).They were on boards with special knives. There was a bowl of pink things which I was unsure about so did not eat but someone told me they were new-fangled prawns.

THE FOURTH GENERATION

Grandmother always made the biggest pork pie at Christmas so everyone would have plenty. I had tried to help her do this once but had been confused about the pastry, you boiled the water and then apparently flung the flour at the water and beat the resultant gloop very, very hard.

There were cakes and trifles and puddings galore. I could make a mean trifle on my own (without cake in, never put cake in) but I was worried about anything made with choux pastry. I understood the boiling water stirring part. However putting 6 egg yolks in the mix sounded very wasteful to me. We only bought six eggs to last us the week in our house. I know that you can use the whites for meringues but I thought that was rather too much stirring and whisking for small arms.

As I stood and looked at this bounty I suddenly had a sense of myself as a separate human being who could make choices. In our house food was something to be tolerated not a delight for the senses. Everything was cut small and delivered in very small amounts. Everything had to be accounted for and no pleasure was to be derived.

My mother was still very, very slender. I had heard people whisper about me behind their hands "She's built just like her father." They were right, broad shoulders, large feet and solid that was me. It had taken until I was nine but I was officially bigger that my mother.

As I stood that day surveying the table, thinking I could make choices, I decided that when I grew up I was going to make delicious food every single day of my life.

CHAPTER 23
Buddy Holly is Dead

School was going really well and I enjoyed it. I liked Mr Smith our teacher, he made learning fun. There were lots of children of my age now and so the school had expanded the only way it knew how, by building prefabs.

Prefabricated buildings were made at factories after the war. They arrived on site ready to be used as houses, offices or classrooms.

THE FOURTH GENERATION

In February 1959 my class was running into the main school building from its prefab. I had learned to run a bit faster and keep up with the rest. We always ran because it was usually raining in Manchester This particular year though had been very, very foggy and caused lots of problems for everyone including my father in getting to and from work

Suddenly we all ground to a halt and a few of the girls burst into tears. As we stood around in a huddle the word went out. Buddy Holly had died in a plane crash at twenty two years old. Then we all burst into tears and were inconsolable. Mr Smith came looking for us and found forty very sad children. His face said that he really had no idea who Buddy Holly was.

About this time I realised that my mother looked very sad. I plucked up the courage to ask her what the matter was and she said" I am just so weary".

Just after that delightful Christmas Hester had fallen on her way to work. She announced that the fall "had taken the stuffing out of her" and she proceeded to sit down in her best chair with the antimacassars. She sat with her feet on a small pink stool. She asked my mother to help her with her cleaning as it was a big house full "of your untidy brothers"

Mona agreed she would go twice a week and clean Hester's house until her leg was feeling better. Mother was very unhappy about agreeing to do this but could not say no. Hester knew Mona was a really good cleaner and began to enjoy being a lady of leisure. One day as my sister, my mother and I arrived at her house she asked my mother to sit down. My mother was not keen on being there anyway as it were the Easter school holidays and she had other things to do.

Hester had decided that she could not manage the house and she was going to pay my mother 10 shillings a week to clean but she would have to pay her own bus fare. I was sitting next to my mother and I felt her whole body stiffen but she smiled her agreement. Hester suggested that I could help clean too as I was there and Gillian could sit with her and keep her company.

As we climbed the stairs I saw my mother brush away a tear but smiled at me when I asked if she was Ok. Hester's fourth son Jeffrey was the only bachelor in the family and still lived at home. Jeffrey was the only child that dared tell his mother what he thought. He had been a pupil at Manchester Grammar School where he told everyone his only sibling were the brothers who were there with him.

He had been in the army in Egypt and had a tan to go along with his receding blonde hair. He had two real bones of contention.

Evacuated as a small child to wealthy, kind people who gave in to his every need he came back after the war exceedingly spoiled. He resented his younger brothers and sisters and could not understand why his parents had not stopped at five children.

I asked my grandmother about contraception just before I was married. "Contraception was never spoken about in our house. A neighbour once suggested Frank wear an overcoat and I never spoke to her again" was all she said. I asked her why she continued to have a physical relationship with Frank when she was obviously worn out from having so many babies. She looked at me with incredulity and said, "He was just gorgeous and I adored him."

Jeffrey's main bitterness went back a lot further. He had been a year old and his brother three when Hannah came for that fateful visit years ago.

She had seen that her daughter was struggling and offered to take one child for a holiday to help her. Hester chose the baby and Hannah was packed to take him on the train with her. At the very last minute she changed her mind and took her baby back and handed her the three year old. In fact from that fateful moment their fates were sealed.

Jeffrey got to live in a house with eight brothers and sisters with all the noise and struggle and absolutely resented it. He felt his real life had been stolen by a brother that was brought up as an only child with wealth and privilege He treated his whole family with disdain at that time. Hester's reaction to this was to treat him like a King. When I went shopping for her as I often did I had to ask the butcher for six pork chops and a nice piece of fillet for our Jeffrey.

He never spoke to me and I had never been in his room. When we got to the top of the stairs my mother stared at me for a moment and the said, "You do Jeffrey's room I will do the rest." She handed me a yellow duster and some lavender polish. "You will not need the sweeper," were her last words to me as she disappeared into her sister's bedroom and shut the door firmly behind her.

As I opened the door it creaked loudly and gave me a start but what I saw intrigued me. There were thousands of newspapers, magazines and books piled up to the ceiling where ever you looked. Empty bottles in every colour where piled in every corner. I could not see the chest of drawers at first but as I climbed over the papers I could see jars filled with pens that didn't work' pencils with no lead and every toothbrush he had ever owned. As I picked them up I decided to count them. The brushes were as flat as it was possible to be. "How hard does this man cleans his teeth I thought." There were 47 used toothbrushes. Light bulbs and bits of engines filled up all the available space and as I looked around I realised that bed was the only space that was not covered.

I sat on the bed for 30 minutes wondering how I was to clean this lot. I finally came up with an ingenious plan. I dipped the duster in the sweet smelling polish and waved the cloth all around the room. I tried to remember my ballet steps as I flung my arms this way and that to dissipate the scent.

When my mother knocked on the door I came out with a smile. I thought, "I can do this on a regular basis as nobody goes into Jeffrey's bedroom and he never speaks to the rest of the family." I was sure my lackadaisical cleaning plan would never be discovered.

On the bus home I secretly hoped she would give me a three penny bit for helping with the cleaning but she kept the ten shilling note to herself. I heard her crying that night and telling my father that she would find a way out of this terrible situation.

My parents had always voted Labour and my father was becoming more left wing. He had become the shop steward at work and with that appointment his self-importance grew. In October of that year there was a general election the Conservatives got in again for the third time.

Macmillan was prime minister and to add insult to injury he signed the European Free Trade Association agreement. My parents were not only socialist they were also anti-European. I was getting to an age when their views on the news began to matter to me.

THE FOURTH GENERATION

However what mattered more was my involvement with the church. I went to Bible classes after school and had developed an encyclopaedic knowledge of religious history.

The only other thing that happened to me was as a consequence of my brain and my feet thing again. My feet were now size 8 and tripping me up wherever I went. I fell on the gravel coming home from school and had a big hole in my right knee. My father on being told what had happened insisted on "having a look". I sat on the edge of the bath and he poked around in it with the flannel soaked in Dettol. I was a very stoic child but this hurt like mad and I screamed accordingly.

My mother had a policy that you did not bother the doctor until something was "about to fall off". Within about four days the teacher suggested to my mother that it was "about to fall off." This was all the prodding she needed and the doctor described a poultice and pink antibiotic. He also suggested I stay off school.

This was a problem for Mona as I was the only child in the school with a never absent never late record and that was not about to be broken.

She came up with a plan with the teacher. I was to be allowed to go in ten minutes late and come home ten minutes early. I was walking so slowly anyway that the kids got home before me anyway. The infection lasted a long, long time and I still have the hole in my knee.

I had a niggling worry about my little sister. Here little knees knocked together alarmingly and the doctor made a hospital appointment. When the date arrived my mother said "here is the card, that is the number of the bus you need to get on and the lady at the desk will tell you where to go."

We were at the hospital most of the day and when we got home she had the most enormous pair of built up shoes. What a pair we must have looked as we walked home.

As the year drew to a close I thought about next year and the 11 plus exam. I knew I had to pass otherwise she would be so disappointed. Little did I know it would be the least of my worries?

CHAPTER 24
We go to Bed early on New Year's Eve in this House

My parents did not celebrate New Year's Eve and went to bed about 9 pm the same as any other evening. This was the first year that I felt as though "something should be happening." At school I had heard tales of staying up very late and jolly parties. There were also stories of dark haired uncles being sent out with a loaf of bread and a piece of coal to let the New Year in. That was regarded very unfavourably in our house.

This was the first time I began to wonder who set the rules that we all had to obey.

Was it God?

Was it the government?

Or as I really thought was it Grandmother Hester?

I did not have an answer. Life had improved immeasurably for me as the big girls from next door but one had lost interest in "coming to take me out".

My mother had always been a manic cleaner. We lived in the tiniest space but she had her hands in water and bleach until her fingers were red and sore.

If it was her kitchen cleaning day she put the red Formica table behind the door and told us to play in the living room until the floor was dry. Every kitchen floor in the land was cleaned and then newspaper put down for at least an hour. If she cleaned the bedroom she would push the wardrobe behind the door and tell us to read until she had finished. This could be hours and hours before she came out. I just thought I was lucky to have such an industrious mother.

I really believed that if the Queen was to come to our neighbourhood that we would be chosen to meet her as our house was so clean. We also had a Cyril Lord carpet and most people had lino and I felt that put us a cut above.

I knew that my mother had always been quiet and thoughtful but this year I felt something was seriously wrong. I knew I was taking my 11 plus in February and so I tried not to think about it too much. I also knew that my father was no longer doing overtime because of his union duties and I wondered if that was the problem.

THE FOURTH GENERATION

One night I woke up and heard the most awful shouting. As a child I had slept very fitfully and woke up at the slightest sound. My parents were in the kitchen yelling at each other. I wondered whose house I was in because my parents never, ever yelled at each other.

That night began a pattern that went on for a while. My father would go with his friend Geoff for a pint after work. I think I heard the name the Sugar Loaf. It sounded like a very bad place to my ears. He would come home drunk and there would be a row.

My mother devised a signal for me. The signal was that she would turn the cold tap on twice in quick succession. There was a problem with the tap and it resounded like a bullet around the small flat. That was my cue to run into the kitchen and at that point she would dress him down for spoiling my chances of passing the eleven plus and going to grammar school because I could not sleep.

This commotion was going on when I was sent to Manchester High School for girls to take the exam. It was a long way on my own on the bus. It is a highly academic school and I really wanted to go there as my aunt Amy had been. Unfortunately it was not to be as I failed by a couple of points. I often wondered how different my life would have been if I had got those points. I was not too worried as I was sure I would pass the 11plus and I heard the new grammar school had boys!

One February night I heard the tap signal and ran into the kitchen only to discover them wrestling. I was swiftly dispatched back to bed. At the time I thought they were fighting and I was very confused. Later I thought that maybe that she had turned the tap on to make him a cup of tea. In my heightened state I had mistaken one turn of the tap for two and that the wrestling had been of the making up variety.

Father stopped going for a drink after work but Mother's mood did not improve. We had a little fold up Formica table and three fold up red chairs. Mother had a little stool which she had covered with Formica to match the chairs. The stool sat beside the table and in front of the cooker. It was a small space and only she could fit in it.

She sat there for hours looking unhappy. She always stroked her chin, whilst smoking one of her Senior Service and stared into the middle distance. I wondered what I could do to help her and I was soon to find out. She was still cleaning for Grandmother and she absolutely hated it. She was such a private woman and she felt that her mother overpowered her.

We had a quiet Easter. Our headmistress was very religious and insisted in going into great detail about the crucifixion. Every year some of the most sensitive girls would burst into tears at the terror of it all. Once she had started she would not stop until she finished with a flourish. "Nobody is to breathe a word of this to the younger children and if I hear that anyone has there will be serious trouble"

Coupled with the fact that all that was on the radio was serious music on Good Friday I grew up thinking Easter was not to be enjoyed at any price. It was true that Gillian and I received about 20 Easter eggs each as we had all those relatives.

The fact that the Easter chocolate was doled out bit by bit took all the fun out of it. My favourite thing though the golden daffodils that were blooming in everyone's garden. I loved the fact that looking at something so beautiful could make your heart sing.

CHAPTER 25.
Cauliflower Cheese for Tea

One night my mother was sitting on the stool looking at me. I had cooked the tea, bacon and cauliflower cheese as it was my favourite thing at the time. She had washed up and I was drying. I think a little moan escaped my lips when I was doing the dratted plastic bags. Well she just erupted with tears, hysteria, shouting the lot. I had never seen her like this. All she kept saying was "You are going to do a lot more around".

"Well actually" I said to myself in my mind "I think I do quite a lot anyway, perhaps Gillian could be given a few jobs" I felt so worried about her and eventually managed to get her onto the sofa. I ran to make a cup of tea. She always took two spoons of sugar in her tea but I thought it was an emergency so I put three spoons in just to be sure.When she finally stopped sobbing she managed to say "I am having a baby". Well fireworks started going off around my head. I was delirious, I loved babies. This news was amazing, fantastic, and joyous.

I looked back at her and realised she was still sobbing. I ran back to put my arms around her and as I dried her tears I whispered "whatever is the matter'" "I am far too old" she said. She was only thirty five years old. I wondered then if it was because baby sister Amy who was twenty three yrs. old and back from Canada was also pregnant.

She absolutely swore me to secrecy. My sister was not to know, my school friends were not to know and no-one in the family was to know. The baby was to be born in November and I was desperate for a brother. Much later I realised that the baby must have been conceived the night of the wrestling match!

As Mona began to get used to the idea she realised that this meant she could stop cleaning for her mother. She had stopped smoking and her family had begun to realise that something was the matter. She let a small delighted circle into her secret but as she insisted on wearing her herringbone swagger coat in all weathers.

I had sat my 11 plus and the day the postman came with the results I ran to hide in the shed. As I was sitting amongst the gladioli bulbs and the flower pots I heard my father shout "Its ok you can come out now" Everyone was very pleased I had passed and now arrangements had to be made to buy the uniform. I had a place at the local co-educational grammar school and there were two shops where you could buy the uniform.

One was Chatterton's in the suburbs where most kids went and the other was Henry Barry in St Anne's Square where the rich kids went. As the uniforms were the same but different, everyone could tell from the day you started which side of the fence you belonged on.

My embarrassment was compounded by two things. It was not the fact that my mother was wearing a grey herring bone swagger coat in a heat wave. It was the fact that she explained to the assistant that she was not paying £2 for an inferior jumper when she could knit one herself. Listening in to this conversation was one of the meanest girls in my class and for some reason I had told her about the baby.

I was petrified she was going to spills the beans. I thought the day could get no worse when the assistant came back to tell the shop in a very loud voice that they did not stock hats large enough for my head and it would have to be specially made. In fact two would have to be made one in pale blue and one in grey velour. The hats were like extra-large riding hats and looked crazy in either colour.

The blue shirts with maroon tie went under a maroon gabardine pinafore. The pinafore had to last for five years. I looked down and thought even allowing for the growing room purchase, there was bound to be a colossal tussle between the stiff gabardine and my alarmingly expending chest.

CHAPTER 26
Summer Feels Good this Year

That summer with its glorious, never ending sunshine felt good. Aunt Amy had given birth to the first grandson in the family and we were all hoping that our baby would be a boy too. I did not agree with my mother's decision not to tell my seven year old sister about the baby. Mother was quite emotional whilst she was pregnant and shouted a lot more than she normally did. I was in a quandary as I really wanted to tell my sister but I knew she could not keep it to herself. As a result poor Gillian got the blame for everything and she did not know why this was.

In the autumn I started at grammar school and got a detention on the second day. It was for the thing I was always in trouble for, talking. I could talk for England. I was afraid to tell my mother but I secretly considered it a more civilised form of punishment than that had been offered at junior school. I had been hit on the hands three times at junior school for talking. It was always a man teacher that administered this. One had to stand in front of him with one hand in front of another whilst he whacked you with a slipper. No matter how much you cried or pulled your hands away at the last minute you had to stand in front of the class until it was administered.

I liked senior school and could not wait for the arrival of the baby. My mother had a perfect pregnancy and was taken into hospital and we were told we just had to wait for news.

THE FOURTH GENERATION

We were having lunch at Grandmother Hester's house when there was a knock on the window. This was frowned upon by Hester and she looked very cross, however when she opened the door it was Grandmother Alexandra who had just come from the hospital with the news that we had a brother who weighed eight pounds. There was great excitement that day. My mother fell madly in love with this beautiful boy and my father was delighted with his son. As the year wore on I got used to doing homework and changing nappies in equal measure.

My mother still was not very well. She was not eating and looked very pale. Everyone who stopped her to look in the pram assumed she had adopted the little boy because she had stayed so slim. One day she took the baby in the pram to the shops she walked home. Her habit was to put the kettle and make a cup of tea before she took her hat and coat off. She was still dithering about when my sister got home from school.

My sister had brought a friend home to see the baby. My sister and her friend ran into the living room and ran out again shouting, "Where's Harry?" Mona was famous for her non expletive expletives and shouted "flipping kippers" as she ran for the door. The baby was where she had left him by the railings outside the greengrocers and he was none the worse for his two hour ordeal.

Things were changing in our house and in the world about us as 1960 drew to a close.

CHAPTER 27
Youth Club and All That

Life was changing; you could feel it in the air. Radio Luxembourg could just about be heard on the radio in the living room We had to listen to it very quietly to avoid father's wrath.

My sister and I would perch either side of the radio in our baby doll pyjamas with our ears pressed against the speaker. We felt very cool until the authorities came in to admonish us for sitting on the expensive sideboard. I did have problems with the living room furniture. One I knew about and the other I did not remember.

The one I remembered was breaking the expensive lamp that was on top of the television. I had leaned across to switch over to ITV. This involved turning a button on a big grey box that sat on top of the very large cabinet. I had somehow over-balanced and burned my arm on the hot bulb in the lamp. This was nothing compared to the burning shame of breaking the expensive lamp.

The other trauma had happened long ago when I was a toddler. They had saved and saved for a bureau. A bureau was a very aspirational piece of furniture that said a lot about you. It sat in pride of place in the living room. According to folklore I had climbed up and taken the key out of the lock and proceeded to scratch the bureau. This incident was mentioned to me every time she saw the scratches: which was quite a lot in the eighteen years I lived at home.

Home life settled into a rhythm and I was enjoying school and youth club. My biggest worry was leaving my little sister behind in my search for freedom. She had been dressed in matching clothes since she was born and came everywhere with me. She came with me to the girls club at the church. We had always gone to bed at the same time. In short she was convinced she was the same age as me. When I went up to youth club she expected to come with me and it just was not possible. Mother suggested I spend another year in girls club but I was making a bid for freedom .Youth club meant excitement and music and fun.

My father's favourite television programme was Wagon Train, Gun smoke and Bonanza. My mother loved Perry Mason and Alfred Hitchcock presents.

We were taken to see 101 Dalmatians at the cinema and we loved Mr Ed on the television. Mother felt that too much television was very bad for children and so we were not allowed to watch it on a Sunday.

Sunday was family day and we always had visitors. Mother dreaded all this work but never dissuaded them.

We also had exactly the same things for tea whenever we had guests. Boiled ham,(always the best quality), tomatoes, (Blackpool for preference), lettuce, (never, ever cress.) radishes, (home grown) cucumber (sliced, pickled in malt vinegar), raspberry trifles, homemade Victoria sponge, emergency shop bought chocolate cake.

In the summer the Granellis ice cream man would fill your bowl up to the top if you ran out to meet him. The ice cream replaced the trifle, heavenly!

We loved our family coming to see us as it was a chance to stay up late. Sonny and his girlfriend Linda were our favourites. He would walk in rub his hands with glee and say "So who are we going to call names then today?" He was such fun and she was so patient. She had beautiful bouffant hair and would let Gillian spend hours combing her hair. She also taught me how to knit and more importantly to hand jive.

Simon and his girlfriend Emma were very sophisticated and drove everywhere in an open top sports car. She was the most elegant woman I had ever seen. She never had a hair out of place and he treated her like a queen. I was totally in awe of her even though she was not that much older than me. Even though on the outside she seemed very formidable I think inside she was very kind.

Gillian and I were bridesmaids at their wedding. My father gave her away at her wedding. It was a small sophisticated affair even though it was in the same church that all the brothers and sisters had been married.

I was actually a bridesmaid to all my mother's siblings. And I had eight bridesmaids at my wedding, the daughters of all my Aunts and Uncles.

Uncle Jeffrey had started to cheer up and turned out to be great fun when he was in the mood. He too had a sports car and drove it with his scarf trailing in the wind as he drove home.

Our most sophisticated visitors were my mother's brother Ned and his wife Hilary. They had never had children and lived in a beautiful house. He was managing director of an engineering company. She was a secretary to someone "high up in the RAF". She had on a fur coat and had a cigarette holder in her hand every time you saw her. They both drank heavily and he died in his early forties.

About a year later she married a retired naval officer who was about 30 years older than her. He moved into her house with his two adult children. About six months after she married she had a brain haemorrhage in a taxi coming home from work and died on the spot. There was a rumour that she was on the way to her solicitors office to change her will. Our other visitors were the sisters who were home from Canada at the time.

My father's sister Jenny also came to visit with her interesting husband Carl. She was a nurse and he was a train driver. He worked five days a week driving trains and two days a week driving coaches. The old ladies on the coach trips loved him as he thought he was Frank Sinatra and serenaded them all the way there and all the way back. Apparently the old ladies were great tippers. He was also keen on canal boats and could draw life like Disney figures. My aunt and uncle had one daughter who was my sister's age. They were desperate for another baby and gave up trying when their daughter was in her teens.

Years later they had a coach holiday in Italy and she came back feeling unwell. They had a lovely little girl twenty years after the first one.

CHAPTER 28
There's a Man in Space

Out in the world things were moving on at a pace. Yuri Gagarin was the first man in space and the Cold War continued to worry us all. The average house price in Britain was £2,500. All my mother's siblings were buying their own house and my mother was desperate to join them.

At home the only low point of the year was when Harry went missing. One morning it was pouring down as I set off on the two mile walk to school. Harry could only just walk when Mother left him stood at the back door watching the rain. She turned her back on him to refill the washing machine and when she looked back he was gone. The neighbourhood turned out in force and eventually the police were called. He was found three hours later near my school and no-one could imagine how he could have got so far. Thus began years of Harry wandering. Years later my sister and I would be stood dressed to the nines ready to go out on a Saturday night whilst our boy friends had joined the search for our brother. He was just an inquisitive child who loved adventure.

That summer I went on holiday with the church youth club. The stunning house had been left to the Methodist church by a spinster with no living relatives. Her wonderful gesture gave so much pleasure to hundreds of early teenagers taking their first steps into the wider world. What I remember best is sitting on a swing, singing fourteen year old Helen Shapiro's "Walking Back to Happiness" over and over again. As I reached for the sky with my sandal shod feet I could see over the hedge across the flower strewn lane to the blue sea in the distance.

CHAPTER 29
Childhood is Ending

Teenagers had not really been invented in neighbourhood at the start of 1962.One day you were a child and the minute you were twelve you were dressed like your mother. My Sunday best outfit was a navy blue suit that my mother had made for me. There was a white blouse with a little tie at the neck and stockings with a suspender belt. A pair of blue shoes with kitten heels and a blue bag of my aunts completed the outfit. I was as tall as I was ever going to be at twelve.

I was also allowed to wear a little lipstick. The paler the better was the fashion of the day. I spent every night with hard, spikey rollers in my hair as I had learned to backcomb and could make my hair stand up in a beehive. I was still very involved with the church and it provided most of my social life.

Father had bought mother a record player and she chose as her record Acker Bilks "Stranger on the Shore". It reached no 1 in America the very first British record to do so and I was allowed to buy Cliff Richards "Living Doll" as he was my favourite. My sister chose "Jail House Rock "by Elvis Priestley.

Our house was a house of unbreakable rules. Some that made sense others that made no sense at all to me no matter which way I looked at it:-

Do not eat Oranges in the house.
Do not use any perfumed soap as it is bad for you.
Do not run the tap whilst you are cleaning your teeth.
Wash and squash every tin before you throw it away.
Clean every tin and milk bottle with hot soap and water.
Hard toilet paper (Isla) was much better for you than the
        soft stuff.
Everything that goes in the fridge has to date marked.
Take you shoes off before you come in the house.
The only shampoo that is any good is green soap that has
        to be mixed with boiling water and allowed to cool
        before use.
Cheddar cheese is not for eating only cooking.
Do not boil more water than you need.
Do not buy apples from South Africa.
All produce must be checked before purchase.

Of course a lot of Mona's ideas seemed crazy in the 1950s and 1960s but many are main stream now.

CHAPTER 30
My Mother the Environmentalist

My mother was thin as a rake, naturally blonde, a wonderful dressmaker, aware of the environment decades before anybody else. She had also begun to take a passionate interest in world affairs. She read the *Guardian* from cover to cover and read nothing but the historical and political tomes she borrowed from the library. She was born before her time.

In the spring of 1962 Harry was just walking and Gillian was eight. She was a very studious and well behaved. Destined to be the headmistress she became, she alternated between a beaming smile that could melt you heart and tears.

Mother had been getting thinner and thinner since Harry was born and in my excitement of growing up I did not realise how poorly she really had become.

THE FOURTH GENERATION

I arrived home to some raised voices coming from the bedroom. Hester had arrived for an unannounced visit and realised my mother was at deaths door. She had stopped eating and had pneumonia. My father was in bed because he was working nights. She got him up and put Mona in bed and sent for the doctor.

The doctor arrived and weighed her and she was less than five stone. I watched in horror as the ambulance men arrived and wrapped her in a red blanket and took her away. I clutched my brother and sister to me as my grandparents walked out of the house and left us with father. He sat on the sofa with tears in his eyes

He began to process information "I do not even know where the vacuum cleaner is kept." He was quiet for a moment and then said, "I can't cook anything and I have to go to work, if I do not go to work we will not eat and I am on nights for the next four weeks. I don't even know where they have taken her." He began to cry and I made him a sandwich. "Can you manage, you will have to manage?"

So within the hour I had ironed his shirt, made his packed lunch and sent him on his way.

I was twelve and I was responsible for a toddler and an eight year old and so it remained for the next eight weeks. The only person that really helped us was Susan's mum who lived next door. We had a top loading washing machine that I could use and I knew how to peg laundry on the line. Susan's mother took the laundry off the line, ironed it and brought it back and she did that for a full eight weeks.

The only mishap was when she fell flat on her face whilst coming round the back of the shed and the clean laundry all fell in the mud. She dusted off her knees picked up the muddy load and took it back into her kitchen. I think she had a heart of gold.

Other than that I had to grow up very fast. My father sent a letter in to school to say I could not go in because my mother had been taken into hospital. No-one from school came near for the next two months. The day I went back they just smiled but something had changed and I no longer felt like one of the clever kids.

CHAPTER 31
Please Keep that Baby Quiet

We got into a routine as my father was working nights. I would take the baby out each day for a walk. I had to keep the house quiet so he could sleep and then go back to meet Gillian from school. We would walk back together and I would make tea before father went to work. It was a good job that I was by that time a good cook.

We really did not know what happened to our mother so we were all very subdued. Father had a phone installed but had a lock put on it so nobody could use it but him. We discovered that they had taken her many miles away to Monsell Hospital. When we asked what was wrong we were told Pleurisy, which not mean anything to me.

Every day was long and boring. I was twelve years old and desperate to see my mother. I tried doing the best I could but it was all I could do to keep up with Harry as he was running around all the time. Whenever I put him in his cot he climbed out again. My little sister was an angel and went to school every morning without a fuss.

I must admit I was very scared at night and slept with the light on in the bedroom. When the baby woke up at night I would put him in bed with me and lie awake worrying whether I would ever see my mother again. We were allowed once to go with father to wave to her from the window. All that did was send the baby and my sister into floods of tears. The building was a Victorian hospital, large and grey and haunted my dreams. My twelve year old brain however could not understand why people did not help us.

I can honestly say something in me shifted at that time and I felt responsible for the world. My grandmother Hester came once and scolded me because the living room floor needed hovering. I am afraid my adoration died a little that day. My other grandmother Alexandra came twice, smiled and left again. I had expected nothing of her and I was not disappointed

Only one of my mother's sisters was in England. Her youngest sister Amy had returned to Canada and her sister Jane were still there. Her sister Beth had returned from Canada with a lovely new baby but was pregnant again and feeling really ill.

THE FOURTH GENERATION

Finally mother came home and she was almost unrecognisable and all she did was cry. She looked in every cupboard and drawer and complained bitterly about the mess. Her baby did not recognise her and just clung to me. It took us a while to get back to where we had been before. She needed to take back the reigns of her life and I needed to get back to being a twelve year old.

Mother finally got better by baking. She loved Mary Berry and had all her recipe books. She began to bake and I think that helped her turn the corner. She made egg custards, chocolate cake, ecclesia cakes, apple pies and meat pies and slowly but surely she began to gain weight and get back the sparkle in her eye. She drank a bottle a of stout every night. She hated the taste of alcohol but the doctor insisted.

When she was well enough Father took her to see West Side Story which had won best picture at the Oscars. My father was becoming more political and there was much discussion about America's blockade of Cuba.

At the end of that year father got a new job. He was made a rate fixer which made him quite unpopular with his former colleagues. He was working more and more for his union and it took up a lot of his time.

About that time my clever, serious and still very frail mother took a job cleaning the local school in a morning. This meant for her that she left the house a six am every morning and came back at 9.30am. It meant for me that I got up as she left and tidied the kitchen and made the packed lunches. I then got my sister out of bed persuaded her to get dressed. By that time baby brother was up and about. I put him in his high chair and left my sister to give him breakfast as I ran to get ready for school. I popped my school bag on my back, made sure Gillian had her things and ran to take Harry to the lady next door who would look after him until 9.30. I then took Gillian to school and then ran as fast as I could to school. That routine continued and I really thought my mother was just marvellous for going out so early to help the family finances.

Mother did try to persuade father to do a little more around the house as she realised he had no skills in that direction. She had always done everything for him and he said "I like it that way thank you."

THE FOURTH GENERATION

Feminism was still some years away from our neighbourhood.

CHAPTER 32
The Kiss in the Dark

The air around me was cold and silent. I could hardly make out what was in front of me and was fighting the urge to scream. I knew my friends were around me but I could not hear anything. As I moved my feet I could feel water sloshing about and the rock I was sitting on felt very cold and clammy under my hands.

I was thirteen years old and on a potholing trip arranged by the church youth club. There were no adults with us on these occasions just a dozen or more fourteen and fifteen year olds. I was definitely the youngest but as my friend Kathleen was two years older was sensible and so I was allowed to go with them. By this time I had a Saturday job helping in a cake shop and so I could afford the train fare.

We gathered early at the train station and bought return tickets to Castleton station. The train was packed with young people as potholing was the thing to be seen doing in 1963. I really, really hated going down dark caves and although I did not have a name for it, I had terrible claustrophobia.

As I sat quietly wondering what to do next I felt someone sit down beside me and brush my hand. "Are you alright" whispered Ken. He was the heartthrob of the youth club and at fifteen one of the older boys. My heart almost stopped beating as I felt him put his arm round me. I had lots of friends who were boys but this was something completely new. As he drew me to him I could not say a word, it was taking me all my time to breathe. He put his lips on mine very gently and my head just spun with a sensation I had never felt before. I did not know what it was but I liked it. Suddenly as it started it was over. He grabbed my hand and said "Come on kid, let's find the others"

In the next few hours my fear of potholing had disappeared as I had a much bigger worry on my mind. How was I keep from my mother the fact that I had been kissed?

THE FOURTH GENERATION

When we finally got back home all the lights were out because everyone was asleep. I crept into the bathroom and put into action the plan I had formed on the train journey home. I was going to put neat antiseptic liquid on my lips because that would the kill the germs that were multiplying on my lips. Every moment counted as I poured the liquid into my hands and slathered it liberally on my lips. It stung a little bit but I was so tired I just fell into my single bed under the window.

Well, the next morning my little sister took one look at me and screamed. She was in the top bunk and my little brother was in the bottom bunk. The noise startled him and he started crying. My mother ran in and her eyebrows shot up. "Come with me" she said and marched me into the bathroom. What a sight awaited me in the small round mirror that father used for shaving, there was a bright, red circle all around my mouth. My lips were cracked and sore and I looked a complete mess. I had to confess all to her and it was one of the few in my life I really heard her laugh out loud. It was a lovely tinkling sound and made me smile through my tears. "You are just going to have to walk around like that like that until it heals"

So I did walk around like that for weeks. Not only did I know I had my first kiss so did the whole neighbourhood.

I do not know if one thing led to the other. A friend from school told me that her parents were going to see the evangelist Billy Graham as he was coming to Manchester.

Louise asked me if I would like to go with them. Her parents were very interested in her life and were always taking her and her sister on cultural visits. This time her sister was considered too young to go on this outing and I was offered her place.

I walked round to their house for a lovely tea and then we set off for Manchester City Football ground. There was a palpable air of excitement as we went through the turnstiles. By the time Billy Graham came onto the stage the crowd were very excited. When he finally asked who would give their life to God I rushed forward on to the football pitch with everyone else.

The excitement lasted until about half way home and I started to wonder exactly what that meant. I hoped it meant doing good works rather than becoming a deaconess. Sister Elizabeth, who was our deaconess, was actually having a tough time with the boys at the moment. She was round and cheerful and never lost her composure. Recently though she had come close to it. She had purchased a "Bubble Car" in which she could just about squeeze her ample frame.

The three-wheeler Isetta car allowed her to perform her duties in the neighbourhood. It would have allowed her to get around faster if she could find it. The boys at the youth club had discovered that if four of them heaved at the same time they could not only lift it off the ground, they could run round the corner and hide it from her.

The first dozen times were amusing but then she began to get very tearful. The vicar called a meeting at the youth club and we were all implored to behave otherwise the youth club would close and that was the end of that.

During this year I had been on a few dates but the one that stood out in my mind was to see the Beatles at Hardwick Apollo. Dave Sharron had got tickets and we had a fantastic evening. John Lennon had replaced Cliff Richard in my affections and I was very excited. In actual fact we were very high up and could not see them very well. In common with every other audience we all screamed so loudly that nobody could hear anything anyway. The feeling of being in the same room as John Lennon was amazing. I guess all the screaming and shaking of heads added to that whizzing feeling as well.

Music and fashion were beginning to change my friend's expectations of entertainment. Instead of going for a walk or to the cinema like generations before, women were now free to go out on their own to dance. The youth culture had started a few years before with rock and roll and everyone had learned to jive but for that you needed a partner. The music of Jerry Lee Lewis, Chuck Berry, and Eddie Cochran and of course Elvis had everyone on their feet in the dance halls. The sight of my friend's older sisters going out in their huge skirts and backcombed hair was amazing. Sugar dissolved in hot water not only stiffened your net underskirt it could be used as hair lacquer in an emergency.

We went out every weekend and sometimes during the week to hear bands play at local church halls. The new dance steps meant that women could dance on their own in groups of two or twenty two .The songs that got most people up was "The Locomotion" by Little Eva, "The Twist" by Chubby Checker and" Do you want to Dance" by Cliff Richard.

CHAPTER 33
The Sixties are Amazing

Manchester was an amazing place to be in the early sixties. In fact it was breathtaking, astonishing, stunning, and incredible, a starburst of sounds, sights and feelings. Every day was brand new like a birthday present waiting to be opened. Excitement pervaded the air around you as you went about the most mundane of tasks in your daily life.

Wayne Fontana and The Mindbenders, Herman's Hermits, Freddie and the Dreamers and the Hollies came to our local youth club to perform. We danced until our feet hurt and walked home in bare feet.

I was very fortunate that my mother only had to look at an outfit in a magazine or on the television and she could replicate it for me. I had some fabulous clothes. I had to buy my own shoes from my Saturday job money however as I managed to get through a pair every month. I was described as "heavy on my feet" but I felt as light as air as I danced the weekend away.

I recently saw a photograph of my thirteen year old slender self and thought "Gosh, perception really is everything ."

My Aunt Jane returned from Canada with her handsome husband Jack. They had bought a very large house and had it converted into lovely apartments. They did not have children but adored me and my sister. I began to spend a lot of time with her. Although she had worked in the film industry in Vancouver she was a skilled seamstress. One day we had a girl's day out and she took me into Manchester to buy some peach georgette. She made me my first real grown up evening dress. Wearing that dress was the first time I truly felt beautiful. I was doing ok at school and starting to enjoy some freedom.

Freedom needs to be in the heart as well as the head and the fact that my mother was feeling better was a great relief to me.

She said to me all my life "Why, oh why do you feel as though you are responsible for the world." I could not tell her why this was so, I only knew deep in my heart the world was my problem. I did not know if I worried because I could not sleep or I could not sleep because I worried. Which every way it was, I spent many sleepless nights tossing and turning putting the world to rights.

CHAPTER 34
The Boy Cycled Straight into my Heart

I was dancing with my friends to music from a new group. The hall was dimly lit but I could see the lead singer in the spotlight. He looked dreamy and I was glad we had decided to walk two miles to a different church hall.

As we danced my friends were convinced he was looking at me but I said, "No he is not." in embarrassment. We had just stopped dancing and had gone for a glass of squash when he sauntered up behind me. "I know you," he said. "You go to youth club with my little sister." I realised he was the famous Dave she was always talking about.

By the time I was fourteen I was tall, much slimmer and thanks to mother's skill dressed in the latest fashion. Short dresses, big hair and pale lips were the order of the day. We all wanted to look like Twiggy. I had inherited my green eyes from great-grandmother Hannah and my dark hair from my father. I spent hours plucking my eyebrows and spitting on a little brush that applied the block of black stuff we called mascara. I always wore the same earrings, big white daisies.

Dave was three years older than me and so we moved in different circles but he was related to someone I knew so that was alright. I was fourteen and when he whispered "I would like to walk you home" I felt quite safe in nodding in agreement.

The rest of the evening was spent in the wonderful knowledge that the blonde, handsome boy who was singing, was singing to me. We began to be inseparable and my friends and I went around all the church halls and schools where he sang. We were convinced that fame was just around the corner. My mother was a little disturbed that he wasn't at the grammar school but was won over by his quiet voice and excellent manners.

That might have gone on for ever except for the boy on the bike. My best friend Anna and I were always together. She was one of four sisters with a much older father. I said to mother that Anna's father always seemed a bit miserable. Her reply startled me" You may as well know now that the older men get the grumpier they get. It's just a fact of life"

Anna confided in me that she really fancied a boy at school. He was in the lower sixth and very handsome. She promised to point him out to me. During the next week several other girls were chatting about how gorgeous he was. One of the braver girls went into his locker to have a look if they could find out more about him as he seemed very mysterious.

I really had no idea who they were talking about as I was so besotted by my pop singer Dave.

On the two mile walk to school I was usually accompanied by friends but this day I was on my own as I stopped to cross the road. As I looked up a boy cycled past me on his bike. He smiled as he whizzed past and my heart stopped. Not only did my heart stop but my legs almost gave way as well. I had been struck by love's arrow and I was never going to be the same again.

I walked to school and as I passed the bike sheds he was putting his bike away and talking to his friends. Anna ran up to me and putting her arm through mine giggled, "That's the boy I was talking about. I am in love with him and so is half the school." As I followed her gaze my heart missed a beat. It was the beautiful boy I had fallen so madly in love with on the walk to school.

I had a terrible feeling that our friendship was going to suffer. I shook my head. What was I thinking, she was my best friend, I was a good person and besides I already had a boyfriend. I could not stop thinking about the boy on the bike. My schoolwork began to suffer, my boyfriend was not happy and my friends were wondering what was the matter with me.

I discovered his name was Grant and we met only once in the next few months. We were both a formal dance with the same school gang. He had a navy suit on and looked so handsome and I had on a pale pink mini dress with a lace ruffle round the neck. We danced in a circle with all our friends and I only had eyes for him. He was dark and slender and was always gazing into the distance.

I finished with my boyfriend and began to mope about. On Easter Sunday I had no plans except to go to church in the evening with my friend Kathleen and my little sister.

As I was passing the phone it began to ring. As I said in my best voice" Mercury 4792" and the beautiful boy asked me out on a date. I could not speak but managed to squeak my assent and agreed to meet him at the bus stop at six pm. However unknown to me, my father had been listening on the other side of the door. He had been having a shave and had happened to catch the conversation.

He came barging through the door yelling but as his face was covered with shaving foam I could not make out what he was saying. As well as foam there was blood as he had cut himself in fury that one of his daughters would agree to go out with a boy she didn't know. Mother came rushing in and there was a frantic search for the styptic to stem the flow of blood.

When everything calmed down she beckoned me into the kitchen. She whispered "You can go, leave the house with Kathleen and Gillian and pretend you are going to church. Please be back by ten pm. I cannot cover for you after that." I think she knew how much I liked him and she approved of him because she knew his mother from the cake shop.

I got smartly dressed but secreted my makeup in my handbag. So off we went, my sister, my friend and a rather uncertain me. I wondered what the punishment was for pretending you were going to church whilst going on a date. We stopped at the paper shop so I could put my makeup on in the reflection. Lots and lots of pale pink lipstick and a tail comb poked in my beehive.

As we waited at the bus stop he walked towards me, a vision in a navy pea coat. My guardians were quickly introduced and then scurried off to church and we smiled at each other. He gently held my hand as we waited for the bus and I thought life will never get better than this. He explained to me that we were going into Manchester to a club called the Jungfrau.

THE FOURTH GENERATION

Walking down the steps into the dark club I realised I had never been anywhere like this and my life was about to change. Beautiful people were dancing to the group. They were called Long John Baldry and the Blues makers and I felt so sophisticated dancing round and around in a circle with him.

We had to leave early as it was time to get the bus home and as he kissed me on the cheek he asked to take me out the following Friday night. As I waved him goodnight I noticed the shadow of Mrs Biddy peering from behind to curtains.

I sneaked round the back into the kitchen and said mother "I think I am in love". She said "Look my love there be lots of boys in your life before you meet the right one". How absolutely wrong she was that night.

Spring moved into summer and my life had changed dramatically. I was no longer going to church, my school work suffered and my friend had really not forgiven me for going off with a boy she really liked.

My mother liked Grant because he was quiet and unassuming and he had no problem with me taking my four year brother with me wherever I went. He also brought me home very early from dates. On a Saturday night we were always back for ten pm and my Aunt Jane remarked that we "said the quickest goodnight of any couple she had ever known"

In actual fact he left very quickly to run to get the all night bus back into Manchester to go to the Twisted Wheel to party the night away with his friends.

CHAPTER 35
I would Like you to meet the Family

He finally took me home to meet his parents. They were friendly enough I suppose. His mother worked at the cake shop and his father was a bus driver. His father was a huge man well over six feet and very broad with massive shoulders. My boyfriend was nothing like him. He was very slender and only weighed about nine stone, in fact had rather an ethereal quality about him.

His mother Laura was another clever woman who had been training to be a pharmacist when she had married his father. She was rather brusque and frightening. Grant's oldest sister Dawn and husband had moved in with her parents whilst she saving up to buy a house. His youngest sister Faith was in my sister's class at school. There appeared to be lots of people in the house. I thought that my mother would never allow so much noise and chaos in her life.

The biggest difference that I could see was that my mother went to bed between eight and nine o'clock and his mother started ironing at about midnight and would still reading a romantic novel at three am.

Someone once said to me "You think your family is normal until you meet another family."

I was so nervous that when she handed me a cup of tea I managed to knock it over and she declared" You are the clumsiest girl I have ever met." I do not think she ever changed her opinion of me!

CHAPTER 36
Whatever is the matter with You?

Walking along a dark corridor in the old building that was The Manchester Eye Hospital, I clutched a bunch of purple grapes whilst chatting to my Billy Graham friend, Louise. Her mother was good friends with the headmistress of our school and I had agreed to go and visit Miss Eaton as she had just had a serious eye operation.

I seemed to lack the ability to say "No." Whatever favour anyone asked of me my brain would be yelling "No," whilst my face would smile sweetly and out of my mouth would come, "but of course"

I really had no idea why I had agreed to accompany my friend as during the last year I had come in for several reprimands from the severe Miss Eaton. However this day she looked vulnerable as she lay between the stark white sheets and she seemed grateful for the grapes and the company.

Two weeks after this visit she returned to school and on the second day I was summoned to her office on the second floor. I waited quite happily, I actually thought she was going to give me an update on her health and thank me for visiting her.

Finally she shouted "Come" and I walked in. The look on her face soon made me realise that I was not there to pass the time of day. I had committed the cardinal sin. Word had reached her that I had been seen wearing the wrong hat. Shame rushed up to redden my hot face. It was true and I could not deny it. The rules were simple you wore your grey velour riding hat from September to March and your blue velour riding hat from April to July. That morning my grey hat was nowhere to be seen. In fact my little brother had been using it to play cowboys and Indians and left it under his bed. The choice was blue hat or no hat and I plumped for blue hat.

As she read me the riot act her tight grey curls bobbed about alarming and the one eye I could see, because she had a patch on the other one, was glaring at me alarmingly. I wondered then as I had wondered many time before why short, round women with grey permed hair and glasses ruled my world.

My grandmother Hester, our neighbour Mrs Biddy, The Guide Leader and the Headmistress were all in charge of my life I had always been a giggly sort of girl but as I got older being reprimanded by someone much shorter than me was guaranteed to set me off. When I started to laugh she got very cross and after awarding me double detention she shouted at me "Whatever has happened to you girl?" I really was not sure what had happened to me. I was trying I really was, but nothing felt right in my world. I did not feel very well but I knew because I had been told, that half the world's work was done by people who did not feel well. I had passed seven mock O levels and was planning to stay on to do my "A" levels. I really, really wanted to be a teacher which pleased the career mistress exceedingly. They were in the business of sending girls into further education from that experimental, co-educational grammar school.

One of the real problems in my life was shoes. Mother and I had made a pact that she would make my clothes if I bought my own shoes. My very large feet seemed to "go through" shoes at an alarming rate. I left my job at the cake shop and got myself a Saturday job at Marks and Spencer's flagship store in town. It was a ten mile journey on the bus but getting up early had never been a problem for me. I took my parents an early cup of tea and caught the seven am bus.

I enjoyed my new job tremendously as I loved talking to new people and it also meant I could afford new shoes and a new coat.

CHAPTER 37
Because You will be Leaving Home Soon

Home life was defiantly getting very cramped as we only had two bedrooms. Mother and father were in the small one at the back and the children had the larger one at the front. The children's bedroom had a pair of bunk beds in which my sister was still sleeping in the top one. She complained nightly about the indignity of climbing up the ladder as she was twelve and very much a young lady. She had begged mother to put our little brother on the top but as he was only five it was considered far too dangerous.

I slept under the window and a chest of drawers filled the room. In fact when one ironed everything had to be folded as we had no hanging room. The only wardrobe was in mother's room and you were only allowed to put your best dress in there

Gillian and I had made a deputation to our mother to suggest we moved to a bigger place but she liked it where she was. The school and shops were nearby and she did not want to change. Her final words on the matter were "Anyway you will be leaving home soon so there will be more room" Mother could have lived anywhere as "neighbouring" was considered a mortal sin in her book. She had a fixed idea in her mind that she repeated often " Children should leave school at sixteen and leave home at eighteen" I really could not understand this as she had stayed at home until she got married at twenty three. It never occurred to me to argue with her. I really hoped I would be allowed to stay on until sixth form.

THE FOURTH GENERATION

Grant, my boyfriend was planning to go to University but had agreed to stay in Manchester so we would not be apart. Mother was becoming more serious and withdrawn and the only way that I could please her was by bringing home lots of nice things to eat from the store.

When the store closed on a Saturday night they sold off all the perishable food. Chicken, Ham, Cream, Mushrooms, Bread and Fruit were all available after six o'clock but it was for a fraction of the price. There was always a long queue that ate into precious dancing time but it was worth it to see her face as she unpacked the bags. Grant had become my ally against the world and would wait patiently outside the store in his new car. Well it was not really a new car. It was an old ford that had cost seven pounds but he was good with engines and it went as long as you did not go more than twenty five miles an hour.

There was really nowhere to do homework in our house. Mother had decided to start making chef's hats from home. This involved the delivery of a huge industrial sewing machine that went under the window where the table had been. Everywhere you looked you could see chef's hats, when you closed your eyes you could see chef's hats. The noise that machine made was horrendous. It clinked, clanked and clonked. There was also white cotton floating in the air wherever you looked and it was attached to all your clothes.

I had actually lost interest in school work. My dreams were of a rose clad home of my own and lots of children. I promised myself my children would be as free as birds.

The disinterest must have been apparent as when the results came I had only got three O levels. There was such a commotion. So many things were said "I was lazy, too interested in my boyfriend" and on and on. I knew that if I was allowed to go back to school I would be alright. I knew that I actually only needed a total of five O levels and a sixth form education to go to teachers training college. All my entreaties fell on deaf ears, I was to go to work and immediately.

My mother considered that the store that I worked at was a good employer and so I was sent to get a full time job. I had actually managed to go the whole of my school life never absent, never late and she considered that great feat. I know I should have argued, stuck up for myself but I had not got the skills or the energy to know where to begin.

I started work the very next week and went to evening college to get my missing O levels. I made a good friend there called Bedelia. She was smart and funny and her life seemed so charmed. I loved her tales of travel and ease. I passed my missing O levels but the ship had sailed and university became a dream for the future.

The only bone of contention was money. Mother was much nicer to me now I was working. I was a fully paid up member of society. I earned £6, paid 7/6d tax and insurance and 12/6d bus fare. That left me with £5 for the week. Mother discussed with me "my keep." It had to be £4, there was to be no argument. I could not make her understand that would leave me with £1 which was less than the money I made working as a Saturday girl. She relented three months later and said I could pay her £3/10s which left me with exactly the same amount of money £1/10s as I had as a Saturday girl

I now had the dubious privilege of spending 40 hours a week standing behind a shop counter for absolutely nothing.

A few weeks later I was serving a customer with a green woollen jumper when I realised it was my history teacher. She looked up from her purse and burst into tears. As I gave her the change she just kept saying over and over "what a shame, what a waste." I liked her but did not care for her husband who was a physics teacher. He had passed me in the corridor one day and said to me, "Your boyfriend would make great ladies hairdresser." "Cheek," I thought as I hurried on my way.

My childhood such as it was, was very definitely over.

CHAPTER 38
Your look very Pale Dear

Blue and red and yellow lights were flashing in my head. I could not see out of my left eye and Lorna who was standing next to me said " You really should see a doctor "I was feeling really ill and had not mentioned it as being under the weather was not

THE FOURTH GENERATION

allowed in our house. One of those dratted rules that had to be obeyed was that you went to work no matter what was wrong with you.

One day in early 1966 I felt really terrible. Mother was still cleaning at the school and so I had packed Gillian off to the grammar school and Harry off to junior school before collapsing back on the bed. I just about had the energy to put my pyjamas back on. Mother arrived home at 9.30 am and had no idea I was in the house. I was fast asleep and so had no idea that she was in the house.

She decided to check that the beds had been made properly and opened the bedroom door. She was so shocked to see her never absent, never late daughter in bed that she screamed loudly. I woke up to hear screaming and a fleeting thought entered my mind that she would make a fuss of me.

However fright turned to rage as she ran to pull me out of bed. "How dare you take a day off you wicked girl, get dressed immediately" with that she marched me to the bus stop. The world was spinning as I waited for the bus to take me on the long ride into town.

By the following week it was apparent nobody could get me out of bed as I just could not walk. I lay there for a week drifting in and out of consciousness, burning hot and not really knowing what was happening. Hester eventually came and demanded the doctor was called.

Dr Simon examined me and declared he did not know what was wrong with me but he thought it might be a new-fangled virus. He would call the next week to check on me. I lay there for another four weeks and they sent an ambulance to take me to the chest hospital for an x ray. They eventually decided it was glandular fever and I would just have to wait until it went.

I was in bed for eight weeks just lying with the curtains closed listening to all the children outside playing in their gardens and wondering if I would get better. Once I began to feel well enough to get up I looked at myself in the mirror and two alarming things had happened. One good one, I had lost so much weight that I had the most amazing cheekbones and one bad one that I was covered in psoriasis. I had the odd spot of this before as it ran in my mother's family but now I was covered in it from head to foot.

THE FOURTH GENERATION

My aunt Jane arrived and declared she would pay for me to see a specialist. It was exactly £5 but my parents did not agree with private medicine The appointment was duly made for me to visit a specialist in St Johns Street. I met her in town and we saw a kindly doctor. He examined me and said "Not only do you have psoriasis but you also have terrible shingles on your back, no wonder you are in such pain". He also declared me to be terribly anaemic and I was to have regular B12 shots for the foreseeable future.

I eventually went back to work and the only interesting thing that happened was that not only did my brother and sister get chicken pox from my shingles, but the majority of the neighbourhood did too.

My boyfriend Grant had been so supportive and had been to see me every day. Although he was at University he had managed to buy a sports car. It was a TR2 and only cost £12and 10 shillings. The reason for the low price was that it had no floor. He spent every waking moment working on the engine and by July declared it fit enough to go on holiday in.

We were going to Newquay in Cornwall with our best friends, Peter and Elaine. Anybody who was anybody went to Newquay that year. We were so excited and were sure we would get there safe even though it was a long journey. Peter and Elaine had a bubble car and so they left the day before us.

Mother had two things to say to me before I left. One was "I still need your keep even if you are going away". She stood with her hand out as I duly opened my holiday purse and doled out £7 of my precious holiday money leaving me with only £4 for the fortnight. The other thing was the only discussion about sex that we ever had "Keep your hand on your halfpenny" she warned ominously.

The journey was divine. I had to keep my legs very still as there was still no floor in the car and when I looked down I could see the road rushing by. There was no roof and so with wind rushing through my hair I felt like a film star. When a downpour arrived and drenched my beehive I felt less like a film star and more like a drowned rat.

When we arrived at the white hill top hotel our friends were already there and had already bagged one of the rooms. I had just assumed that I would be sharing with Elaine and that Peter and Grant would be sharing. I looked at Grant and he looked back at me.

Although it was the sixties, free love had sailed right passed me. A combination of my mother, the church and wanting to obey the rules that "they" had set meant I was very anxious about sharing a room with a boy. I had been dating him for three years but I need not have worried as although we shared a bed he was a perfect gentleman for the whole two weeks. I was to remember that holiday many, many years later.

We had a magical time, sunbathing during the day and dancing in the night clubs at night. It was one of the only times in my life that I felt like one of the really cool people.

"Were you alright, you looked really anxious as you waved us off" I said to mother as I went into the kitchen when I got home "I never thought I would see you again" was her answer.

My little sister was growing fast and proving herself to be a very able student. She did not however like housework and would collapse into hysteria if asked to lay the table. "Homework" was the reason she gave for getting out of any chores and so I just carried on helping as normal. I also still took my little brother Harry with me wherever I went.

Chapter 39
Harold Wilson is in Town

Gillian was turning into a very pretty, slender young woman and spent ages doing her hair. One day we were all going out and one of the aunts suggested that she might look a little better, if she was a little thinner. Gillian burst into tears and the outing was cancelled. "Just what we need in this house," I thought, "another person who will not eat."

Grant took a day off University to take my mother into town to see Harold Wilson. She spent many hours reading about politics and although she was a committed socialist she did not agree with all Wilson's policies. He announced that Britain had applied to join the European Economic Community and she did not agree with this idea. After hearing him speak she agreed that she understood his reasons.

THE FOURTH GENERATION

The whole family had started to watch some television together. Thursday nights were Top of the Pops and Man from Uncle which we enjoyed. Sunday night was the Forsyth Saga which mother enjoyed. The Beatles Sargent Pepper album was being played everywhere.

As northerners we much preferred the Beatles to the Rolling Stones. My mind was changed just a little when a friend's mother got us tickets for Top of The Pops. Dancing round in a circle never felt so cool. The recording studio was in Rusholme and Alan Freeman, David Jacobs and Pete Murray presented the show. As well as The Stones, The Dave Clark Five and Dusty Springfield were on when we went to see the show recorded.

CHAPTER 40
That Wonderful Summer of Love

1967 was the summer of love. The San Francisco hippies with flowers in their hair were the enduring image on the television. Although some of their ideas of idealistic politics did not survive, their summer of love gave way to freedom for the young. Most of the boys in our neighbourhood favoured the mod style of dressing with sharp suits and short haircuts and everyone's father wore a car coat.

My grandmother Hester had been left some money and she bought an Anglia car and a new china cabinet. She had been left a small inheritance by her mother Hannah who had died in her eighties. She had amassed a small fortune in her days as an hotelier and shared it equally between her children.

The other inheritance came from a Danish sailor called Carl. He had come to England after the war and fallen in love with Clara, Grandmother's childhood companion. They did not have children and he promised his worldly goods to my grandmother as she had looked after him after his wife died.

As it turned out when the will was read out there were not many worldly goods left. He had made friends with a young woman who lived nearby and had a wonderful few months spending his money on her. Grandmother laughed when she heard the news and said "There's no fool like an old fool".

Hester loved the car because it meant she could drop in on any of her children at a moment's notice. She was famous for persuading Grandfather to drive her to her chosen victim and then cause a big ruckus and leave again just as quickly. My mother dreaded looking out of the window to see the maroon Anglia outside the house.

Hester agreed she would not drive but insisted on being shown the ropes so she could stop the car if Grandfather had a heart attack. On every journey, long or short, she sat fully braced and at the ready so that at any moment she could lean across turn the key off and pull the handbrake on. To see my well upholstered Grandmother in her best fur coat and hat ready to pounce was the stuff of hysteria and I loved going in the back of the car with them.

I could drive but had not passed my test. Father had taken me out for a lesson at the local shops car park just before my test. Some pigeons had landed just in front of me and I had swerved so violently that I had written off his treasured but extremely ancient Hillman Imp. He insisted in cancelling my test immediately.

CHAPTER 41
Will You please, please Marry Me?

There were lots of different things going on that year. The Beatles and the Stones were in the charts but so were The Seekers with Georgia Girl and Des O'Connor with Careless Hands. The discussion at the dinner table was of Beeching axing the railways and the changes on the Radio.

Mother loved Radio Four and listened to it all day every day for all of her life. Radio one had young DJs like Tony Blackburn but also middle age men with mellifluous voices like Pete Murray. We went to the cinema to see the latest James Bond film but Carry on Doctor was very popular. The other very popular form of entertainment with the everyone was the huge variety clubs that had popped up everywhere. They were very approachable places. You sat at tables of ten or twelve eating your meal and drinking your drinks whilst listening to comedians, classical singers or pop groups.

In May that year my sister Gillian was having a party. This had never been allowed as mother hated people in the house but Gillian wore her down. Mother, Father and Harry were going to the cinema and Grant and I were to be in charge.

That night was momentous for two reasons. She was fourteen that day and met the boy she was to spend the rest of her life with and I at seventeen asked Grant to marry me. I had really had no idea I was going to do it, it just happened.

Gillian begged us to leave the party for a while. She said we were really, really embarrassing her and so I agreed to leave for one hour. We decided to walk to the airport and give her some freedom. It was a lovely evening and we held hands and chatted as we walked.

I knew I loved him so much that I would never want anyone else. I also knew I was so trapped at home that I needed to escape. I hated all the rules that kept us in our place and I was fed up with sharing a room with my teenage sister and little brother who was growing up fast. It was the sixties but I did not know anyone who lived together before marriage. In our family you got engaged, married and had a baby in that order.

As we walked back towards the party I suddenly stopped and blurted out "I really, really want to get married". I do not know who was more shocked me or him. He looked at me for a very long time. He was still at university and did not have a penny to his name. His granddad had given his father £1000 for Grant's education but it had all been spent years before by his parents.

"I don't see why not, but you will have to wait until I get my next grant for a ring". He smiled and my heart did a summersault.

When we got back to the party all was well and the parents arrived home soon afterwards. I could not wait to tell them my news. I was getting married but Grant would have to ask for permission first. Just as he was going to ask father to step outside we realised something else was happening.

"I have some news" said father a little self-importantly. He turned the music off and in one swoop the partygoers disappeared into the warm summer's night.

CHAPTER 42
Father is Going Up in the World

He sat us down to tell us that he had left his job at the factory and had taken a job with white collar union ASTMS (The Association of Technical and Managerial Staff). Fortunately for me he was going to get a company car and so the discussion about the wrecked Hillman imp came to an end. He was destined for a completely different life and my mother would finally get the beautiful house she coveted.

We all congratulated him and there was much excitement. I whispered to Grant "Leave it, ask him tomorrow" So the next day he did ask him for my hand in marriage and he said "yes". We were engaged but I was not going to wait for a ring.

I now worked in the offices at the Marks and Spencer store. Sylvia the girl that sat next to me at work was getting engaged. She was Jewish and so tradition dictated that she would have a beautiful diamond. She agreed to take me with her to see the diamond merchant. We went up in a rickety old lift and knocked on a locked door. A very old man with huge glasses opened the door and we were in.

She was to have three carats and he brought out the diamond she had chosen. It was breath taking and so began my lifelong love of beautiful rings. I explained that I had £42 which was the exact sum of my boyfriend's grant. I knew we would not be going anywhere for the next year but it did not matter.

The jeweller looked around his work bench and handed me a half carat diamond and set he could set it in platinum for £42. I had a picture of a design I liked but the jeweller advised me to keep it plain and told me to come back next week for a fitting.

Two weeks later it was my birthday I was going to be eighteen. That did not mean anything in the sixties as twenty one was the age of consent. I was going to get engaged on my birthday. The day dawned and my friend Lorna and I set off to collect the ring. I had been saving and saving for this ring and counted out the money in small denominations. I thanked the jeweller for my precious possession.

I put it in its box and set off for the Chinese restaurant where Lorna and I were to meet Grant. I was in heaven as he put the ring on my finger. "We are going to get married in two years" I announced. We would have been together five years by then.

It was only years later that I realised that I had asked him myself to marry me, bought my own engagement ring and planned my own wedding. He, sweet man, had just gone along with it. His part in the proceedings had been to turn up for a Chinese meal. I do not think I ever got the £42 from him.

CHAPTER 43
We are All going to a Dinner Dance

My mother's family organised a dinner dance as a celebration. Dinner dances were the way to celebrate anything and everything in the late sixties. There was some tension as both families were there. My future mother in law did not care for my maternal grandmother and thought her "far too dominant" and my maternal grandmother did not care for my future mother in law and thought her "far too opinionated."

Mother did not care for my sister's dress thinking it far too short or for her sister's attitude to "everything". Mother and her next sister Beth really did not agree on anything. Mother thought she had too many airs and graces. Most of the trouble was about smoking as my mother smoked and her sister thought it a disgusting habit. She actually insisted that mother went outside to smoke!

My future father-in-law did not agree with eating out but he did agree with drinking out. He was convinced that you did not know what people put in your food but that drink was unadulterated. I could see him sitting at the bar whilst we were eating. I was convinced that he was drinking something in a small glass every time he ordered a pint. My fiancé said I was imagining it.

I was proved right when he tried to get off his stool and fell flat on the floor. He was a very large man and proved hard to move. The snooty ones in mother's family would have nothing to do with him but some of the younger uncles and his son helped him up. A taxi had to be called and he was packed off home.

THE FOURTH GENERATION

I was engaged and there was a wedding to plan. Even though it was two years away I knew exactly what I wanted. My fiancé was twenty and finishing university. He was very quiet but I made up for that with my ebullience and good cheer. I saw the best in everybody I met and would offer help at any given opportunity and I have no idea why I needed to do this.

I was forging out a career for myself and he was just doing his thing. He had one great friend from childhood who he spent a lot of time with. At the weekend Grant and I had started going to more grown up places like Bredbury Hall. All the clubs in the city centre did not sell alcohol. If you wanted a drink you had water or a soft drink. The more sophisticated places had alcohol but only with a meal. There was chicken a basket everywhere we looked in 1967.

CHAPTER 44
Grandmother Really is not Well

I often had a feeling that although I adored my fiancé I did not really know him at all He got a job as a quantity surveyor and started to work in an office in the city but I think I knew his heart was not in his work life.

In October of that year a bombshell dropped on our family. My darling grandmother Hester on returning from visiting her family had finally gone to the doctors with her bad cough. She was diagnosed with lung cancer and told she did not have long to live. She was in her early sixties and the strong, powerful matriarch just fell to pieces.

There was a family conference and it was decided that someone would have to stay with her. As they looked around the room I felt all eyes settle on me. "No," my brain yelled and my face smiled and I said "Alright I will do it."

I rang work the next day and got three weeks special leave. I packed my bag and jumped on the bus to go to my grandmother's house. When I arrived the house was in darkness and she was sitting in the kitchen by the range weeping silently into her apron. My heart went out to her.

I made us a cup of tea and managed to sit her in her favourite chair and when I opened the curtains I could see there were flowers on every surface. The heavy scent of sweet peas hung in the air. She was such a force in her church and neighbourhood that everyone had bought flowers for her.

I stood with my back to her with tears streaming down my face. I really did not know how I was going to do this. I closed my eyes to say a little prayer but even though I was standing in the shadow of the church nothing came to me. I felt very alone just like I had when my mother was in hospital.

We did manage and in the three weeks I stayed we ate delicious food, we read, we laughed and cried and slowly she began to be able to cope.

We celebrated Christmas with heavy hearts but she lived until the following spring. I was comforted by the fact that I only had one more Christmas at home before I got married and could begin my own grown up life.

CHAPTER 45
Mother, Have You Moved my Stuff?

The following year the news bulletins were still of the Vietnam War and the problems in Rhodesia, later to become Zimbabwe. As Easter approached my future mother-in-law announced there was to be a family holiday "Would we like to join them?" She loved her holidays "they make life worthwhile" she would announce. They were going to Devon for one week and we decided to go with them.

The car we travelled in had a bench seat in the front and Grant, his grandfather and his father sat in the front. His mother, his younger sister, his younger sister's friend and I sat on the back seat.

When we were all packed in I realised it was going to be a terrible journey made worse by the fact that the dog Whisky was being squashed into the old Zephyr. A definite faint effluvia followed him everywhere. The journey was made worse by the fact that the engine kept overheating and we had to keep stopping to let it cool down. We actually had a good time on that holiday and I came back feeling relaxed and calm.

That did not last long as I entered the front door I could feel the changes shimmering in the air. Everyone looked from one to another as if debating whether to tell me something. I handed the presents round and then picked my bag up to put it on my bed and unpack.

When I went into the bedroom it took me a minute to take stock. My bed had gone, but as I looked round so had the bunk beds. In their place stood a double bed in all its glory. I ran into the little bedroom followed closely by mother. "What have you done "I whispered.

The bunk beds had been split in two and stood either side of the chest of drawers. There was also a folded up, foldout bed and a box with all my possessions peeping out in the corner of the room "What have you done,?" I whispered again.

"You know how much I hate this little backroom so we took the opportunity whilst you were away to change the rooms around. "Where am I going to sleep" I whispered with increasing alarm. "You can go on the fold up bed, you are getting married soon," she said in a tight, pinched voice. Soon,! soon! My wedding was twelve months away.

I turned on my heel and ran straight out of the door to Grant's house. We went for a walk and I told him that what had happened and said "What am I going to do, we have to get married" He held me in his arms but did not say a word. Eventually he took a deep breath and he said, "If that's what we need to do, then that's what we will do." He thought for a moment and said" I know, I will sell my car". Well technically it was his grandfather's and my car too.

CHAPTER 46
The Pale Blue Sunbeam Alpine

Earlier on in the year the car with no floor finally gave up and Grant's uncle on his mother's side had agreed to sell him his Sunbeam Alpine. The car was white and shiny and of course the favour meant it was more expensive than if he had bought it at the garage. Grant came to me first "I really want the car, will you go halves with me?" I duly trotted along to the post office but my meagre savings still would not make up the amount. He then went to see his grandfather and he agreed to make up the difference and so the car was duly purchased.

The Sunbeam Alpine was declared fit enough to take us work in Manchester. His brother-in-law was there when the car arrived and asked if he could come with us to the city in a morning as well. Each morning Grant would pick me up and drive to his sister's house. I would step out and his brother-in-law would get into the tiny space behind me. He was a very well upholstered policeman who stood over six feet tall.

The trouble was that as I got back in the car the seat would not go back down properly. I spent many mornings being driven to work leaning forward balanced at forty five degrees. The strain on my arms to keep me balanced left me exhausted. I do not know why I did not suggest that he got the bus.

The trouble was that the car broke down on a regular basis. One morning as we drove along the Princes Parkway the car just stopped. We piled out into the pouring rain. We pushed the car over to a petrol station and the left it to rush for the bus. In the evening we got off at the stop and I stayed at the side of the road whilst Grant walked along the centre of the road. He looked like a detective looking for clues.

Suddenly he yelled and raised his arm above his head. In his hand was a long thin object. He shouted "It's the prop shaft" as he ran past me to the car. Magically he was able to put it on quickly and we were on our way home. I thought he was my knight in shining armour.

A couple of weeks later we had another in interesting incident at that part of the dual carriageway. The road had a wide centre reservation with grass and trees. One sunny morning as he negotiated the roundabout he over steered. The car left the road and mounted the central reservation. We drove the whole of the way to the next roundabout between the trees as though we were on a Sunday outing. At the next roundabout he left the central reservation and returned to the road. No one said a thing but I remember thinking that he would make a great racing driver.

THE FOURTH GENERATION

The next day I went to see the vicar to see if there were any spaces for weddings at the church this summer. The first date was a couple of months away. I quickly booked it and he chatted to me about the sanctity of marriage.

My future mother-in-law was not very pleased stated that thought the whole thing "Far too rushed "There was also a problem with his best friend. Grant rang me to say that he was driving him to the passport office as he had decided to go to Canada. He had then taken him to the port to catch the boat. He had decided to go at the last moment after apparently having a meltdown at Grants house. The reason was supposed to be a "bad trip" but I never knew the whole story. Well, I did but that was years later.

The plans for the wedding went on apace. My tally of bridesmaids mounted daily, big ones, little ones and middle sized ones; apparently I owed everybody a return bridesmaid favour. Mother offered to make all the bridesmaids dresses. I should have stopped at six but another two cousins crept in under the wire the four big ones were to be in pink and the four little ones in white with guipure lace.

As we had changed the dates I had lost my lovely venue for the reception and the only place that could manage 80 guests was a local pub. It was not exactly what I wanted but I was fed up with sleeping between my brother and sister.

Grant had put the Sunbeam Alpine in the for sale ads in the paper. One day a very nice man whose wife was very ill arrived at Grant's house. He quickly agreed the asking price, wrote out a cheque and giving his address drove off in the car. When Grant rang me to tell me about the sale I said "Are you sure that you should have taken a cheque from a stranger and given him the car" He assured me that he seemed a very nice man. Of course the cheque bounced. There was no such address, no sick wife and no nice man. There was also no car and no money with which to get married.

I tried to console Grant as he was very upset. I really wanted to scream and shout but thought he would be even more worried.
Despite having much less money than we had imagined the wedding plans were coming together nicely.

CHAPTER 47
A Young Man from Nottingham Smiled at Me

One day I was introduced to a young man who was working the summer holidays at the store after he had finished his degree at Manchester University. He was an engineer and he was so handsome but more importantly very interesting and amusing. We talked and talked about anything and everything. We started taking our lunch at the same time and sitting in the cathedral grounds whilst we talked about the world. He had travelled a lot with his family and intended to work in America for a couple of years. People at work were beginning to raise their eyebrows but I was not doing anything wrong. I had also told my fiancé about him.

We never held hands, we never kissed. I felt our connection was merely the meeting of minds. I did know however that I was happy when I saw him and he made me feel safe, intelligent and beautiful.

The date of the wedding drew closer and we needed to find somewhere to live. We found a great flat in Stockport. It was airy and bright and just the place to start our new venture together. The man who owned the flat told us that he had a music shop that he had turned into a recording studio. He told us that lots of different pop groups were beginning to record in his Strawberry Studios. He mentioned lots of famous names but the one I remember was10 CC as there were my favourite. One night just before we were due to move in the couple upstairs left a tap on and flooded our flat. We were very disappointed but we found a new house to rent not far from where our parents lived.

My memory of that house is distilled into one bunch of flowers that sat in the glass porch for weeks in pristine condition. There were pink parrot tulips, purple iris and white narcissus in a crystal vase that had been one of our wedding presents. The flowers nodded their heads in greeting to me every morning as I rushed out into the snow. The image of those flowers made my teenage spirits soar and when I close my eyes I can see them clearly now.

I finished work the week before my wedding. Grant came to collect me and just as I passed through the door the handsome engineer handed me a huge bunch of red roses. As I reached the car,

THE FOURTH GENERATION

Grant stepped out and smiled at me and took the roses from me. He walked back across the road and put the roses in the bin. He had seen who had given them to me. We did not speak all the way home. I have wondered how different our lives would have been if we had communicated that day.

Two days later I was having my final fitting of the elegant wedding gown that my clever mother had made for me. It was just divine. It was a silk ballerina column dress and a beautiful guipure lace coat with a long train. Just as I was trying it out for the final fitting the phone started to ring. I was nearest the phone and bent down to pick it up. A voice I knew well pleaded. "I am leaving for France tomorrow. I love you, please come with me". As I glanced up I saw my bride's perfect white reflection shimmering in the mirror.

Through stinging tears I told him I was sorry and that I hoped he had a wonderful life. I knew then that I wanted to go through with my wedding. I loved Grant and I knew my life was meant to be with him. I had never shared any of this with mother. At eighteen I was still obeying no law but mine: "Do not upset your mother!"

As I put the phone down I stared at her with her mouth full of pins. My clever mother was so private that she would not have thought it her business to tell you if your hair was on fire, stared back at me. She took the pins out of her mouth and sighed. "You don't have to do this you know, I have a feeling that your life is going to be hard if you marry this boy."- "I love Grant and would not hurt him for the world" I said through my tears. Then she uttered her final pronouncement "On your own head be it" and went off to make a cup of tea.

CHAPTER 48
A Good Time was had by All

Our wedding day dawned clear and bright. My older bridesmaids and I headed off early to the hairdressers in Manchester and my mother went off to her local appointment.

When we stepped out of the taxi I could see my beautiful coiffured mother with her pink hat perched on her head walking towards us behind the hedge. As she rounded the corner I could see she had on her old, brown anorak and slacks and she was carrying enough fish and chips for twelve people. The nerves and the absurdity of her outfit got the better of me and I had a fit of the giggles. The fish and chips were demolished and we all set about getting ready.

I was in heaven when the flowers arrived in their long cream box. As I gently pulled the tissue paper aside the perfume from the roses and freesias hit and delighted my senses. Everything was going to be alright.

As four pm approached we all looked at each other in anticipation. Then I noticed my little brother Harry. Two months before the wedding I had taken Gillian and Harry into town to have a professional photograph taken for mother's birthday. We had taken the opportunity to buy him an outfit for the wedding as he was going to be a page boy. The outfit we had chosen was a soldiers uniform complete with bearskin hat, red jacket with gold buttons and black trousers.

As he stood to attention beside me I saw that the hat fitted, the jacket fitted but the trousers finished just below his knees. This seven year boy had dared to have a growth spurt! My brother has always been a good sport and it was a good job that day as various ladies in hats tried to pull his trousers up and then down to see what looked best. The answer was nothing looked right so he would have to go as he was.

This little drama meant that the wedding party went off in high spirits and I was left alone with father. We had always had a very close and jolly relationship and everyone had always said we looked alike. He had changed so much in the last year. Important meetings in London and lunches in nice restaurants were what his life was about now. As we stood looking at each other I thought here's your chance take it. I looked him square in the eye and said "You must know how much mother wants to buy a lovely house with a garden you have such a different life now, she deserves her chance as well" We glared at each other for a few moments. "You know I do not agree with property ownership" he said through clenched teeth. "Just think about it" I said as I hugged him.

We left the flat and walked around the square to the taxi. The route was lined with all the neighbours, as was the fashion of the day.

As I looked at all those faces I realised that my childhood was over and I was going to be a married woman.

I was still thinking about the bid I had made for my mother's dreams when we arrived at the church. This was St Andrews the church I had attended all my life so I expected to see a lot of the congregation there.

It took a moment for my brain to compute as I had been flung back in time. All I could see were the boys from my class at grammar school. In the last couple of years they had turned into large men and were all standing about with their hands in their pockets. "Had I invited them?" I thought. What were they doing here?

Then as I stood waiting to go into church another bride appeared from out of the crowd. Had I turned up on the wrong day? I said a little prayer to myself for God to beam me up from the embarrassment. I did not recognise the bride but I did recognise the groom. He came across and hugged me. "Bit of a rush job I am afraid. The vicar kindly gave us the slot before you and we over ran a bit". Martin had been my dear friend since infant school and I knew he had gone to study architecture at University.

My anxiety flew away as we wished each other good luck. I then saw all my wedding party trooping in to the church and I waited a moment for the music to start.

CHAPTER 49
The Yellow Rose in his Lapel

As I walked into the church on my father's arm I saw my gorgeous bridegroom waiting for me. He had on a navy suit from Austin Reed with a yellow rose in his lapel. He has always had the ability to make my heart do somersaults and that day was no exception.

When I looked at him I noticed that he had a very red face with white patches around his eyes. I could not think what it could be as he had promised me that he was going to have an early night before the wedding. He had had a rather sedate bachelor party a couple of weeks before to which the fathers and uncles had been invited. The real bachelor party had been the night before the wedding. I found out later that some fool had decided that it would be a good idea for them all to go to the Turkish Baths on the morning of the wedding. The results are plain to see in the wedding photos.

Well they would have been if the photos had turned out. One of my friends from work had listened to my story of the stolen car and knew we did not have much money. She said "My cousin Jim is a photographer; well actually he is a staff nurse but does photography as a hobby. He has very reasonable rates and is very good"

So Jim took the photos and all I can say is I hope he was a better nurse than he was photographer. The shots were dreadful and only about six pictures came out. I smiled when I paid him and did not have the heart to tell him to stick with his day job.

As I said the vows about honouring and obeying I knew I meant them for life. I said to myself "Remember this day my girl as this will be the only wedding you will ever have" I did however have to contain my giggles when I realised my kneeling new husband had left the price on the bottom of his shoes.

The church was full to capacity but only eighty guests were invited for the wedding breakfast. The rest would come to the dance in the evening. We had a wedding car to take us on the ten minute journey. We did not speak, we just held hands. Some of my pearl buttons had come undone and so I concentrated on trying to fasten them with my one free hand. I think we were both in shock. I looked lovingly across at this familiar stranger and wondered what the future held for us.

The reception proved to be a jolly affair with much laughter and joy. We had an excellent band but the hit of the evening was my friend Susan who had the most beautiful soprano voice. She sounded like Joan Baez and everyone loved her. At about nine pm I went to change before we left the party. I had bought an elegant mustard and brown trouser suit and matching floppy hat. I felt amazing although I did hear one of the great aunts say, "A trouser suit is totally unsuitable for a going away outfit." It was a good job that I was not going very far then!

The house we were renting was about fifteen minutes' drive from the reception. Grant had hired a car for two days and I sat back in the passenger seat with my eyes closed thinking it had been a long day and I would be glad to get in bed.

I had made the little house beautiful. I had spent the last month making the home I had always wanted. Mother had made the curtains and I had bought lots of pieces from junk shops and lovingly sanded them down and painted them. We had received some lovely presents of bed linen and rugs for the sanded floors. I had found an old refrigerator and my parents had bought us a cooker. It would be home sweet home.

CHAPTER 50
My Shattered Wedding Night

I had been to our house the day before the wedding and put flowers on the kitchen table and as I locked the door behind me I experienced a warm glow of satisfaction. This would be a home that would be filled with lightness and joy. If I wanted to eat ice cream at two o clock in the morning then I definitely would. I was so looking forward to getting home and as I negotiated the pathway in the dark I felt something crunch beneath my feet. It was definitely broken milk bottles. Grant's key would not open the door and so he hopped over the fence to try the back door. Maybe hopped is not quite the right word as drink had been taken.

Eventually he opened the door and in the darkness said in a quiet voice "I think we have been burgled". As I struggled to take off my trendy mustard hat I cried "Who would burgle us, we have not got anything" I looked around in the darkness for somewhere to collapse but the chairs and sofa were turned upside down. He came back with the emergency torch he had put under the sink.

By the light of the emergency torch we discovered that someone had taken all the light bulbs out. When we went upstairs realised that every one of the bulbs had been smashed and put in water in the bath tub. When we reached the bedroom we realised that our bed had been completed dismantled and my lovely bedding had disappeared. I slid down the wall to the floor and began to realise that this was not a burglary. It was a prank that had gone too far.

I realised that a group of uncles, brothers in law and cousins had broken into house to have a little fun at the new couple's expense. What started out as a prank had turned into a major ransack. As I peered about at the devastation I thought about calling the police. Then I realised that at least two of the drunken protagonists were policemen and thought better of it. My new husband went to make me a cup of tea and realised that all the food from the fridge and cupboard had been mixed together in a horrible mass.

We spent our wedding night, waiting for dawn with me sitting in the bath and he was perched on the loo as they were the only two seats in the house. I vaguely wondered as the night wore on how many couples really have the romantic idyll that they dream of.

The next morning we set about cleaning up the mess, rescuing what we could and making a list of what we would have to buy. Grant offered not one word of admonishment to the silly men who had done this terrible thing to his bride. It was he said, "just one of those things."

Grant had reported his stolen car to the police but they held little hope of getting it back. Like everyone else they could not believe that he had given his classic sports car to a total stranger without getting the money first. The money for the honeymoon had disappeared along with the conman. When I looked back on that incident I wonder why I was not furious with him. I think I felt quite sorry for him that someone could be so unkind and that set a pattern for our married life. So, as we had a hire car for a couple of days, we decided to drive the 150 miles to Anglesey for lunch. We had ham sandwiches and chocolate cake on the beach. As I sat on a rug looking at my husband I thought I was the luckiest girl in the world.

The next day he had to take the hire car back and I carried on with the cleaning of the damaged house. I managed to save the light shade from Habitat that had been my one major investment. As I was listening to radio one I heard Alan Freeman announce the number one record on the top forty shows. His was the voice of Sunday night radio. His distinctive style included the catchphrases "Not arf", "Greetings pop pickers" and "All right stay bright" That evening the song he played was by the group Marmalade. The title was actually "Obladee Obladaa." To my young ears that evening it sounded like

"Oh Bloody Oh Bloody Ahh!" I wondered if it was going to be the anthem for my marriage.

CHAPTER 51
You've broken my Lightshade

Grant and I took a week off work after the day of our wedding. We had two incidents of note that week and one involved a Spanish radio station. We had a small transistor radio that had to be held a certain angle to get the right sound.

My husband was a committed Manchester United supporter and that week he was determined to hear the match against Benfica. The only way he could get a good reception was to stand on a stool in the middle of the living room. I decided to read a book in the kitchen as I peered through the open doorway I was convinced he was going to do himself some damage balancing so precariously.

I had inherited my mother's taste for reading serious books and was engrossed in a chapter of *On the Road* by Jack Kerouac. I was fascinated by all things American and hoped one day to be able to live there. I loved the story of the Beat and Counter culture generations and the freedom they seemed to represent. My brain was 6000 miles away when I heard a bang, a crash and yell at the same time.

I went running in and it came as no surprise to me to see him lying on the floor. There was blood everywhere and he was clutching his ankle and hopping about. Manchester United had scored and in his excitement he raised his fist. This had caused him to overbalance and he had grabbed my very trendy but very sharp light fitting as he fell. The stool went over, he went over and my lovely shade fell to the ground and smashed.

He was really impervious to the pain as he had been having a few beers as he listened to the match. I took the emergency first aid kit which contained an emergency crepe bandage and some antiseptic and proceeded to put him back in one piece. I could not do the same for my trendy light fitting as it was beyond repair. As I went to the cupboard I thought to myself that the "Millie Molly Mandy" life I imagined for myself was turning into one long episode of *Some Mothers do have Em.*

My opinion was compounded later that week when coming through the front door with a bottle of my favourite wine Mateusz Rose he managed to drop it and it smashed all over the floor covering me in a fine pink spray.

CHAPTER 52
What Have I done Now?

The following Saturday I walked into the new shopping centre that had recently opened. Grant had gone to the football match and I was at a loose end. As I passed the church where I had been married a week before I heard the bells ringing. From the church stepped the milkman's daughter who was marrying the postman's son. It occurred to me then that nobody went far to find a husband.

Grant had finally bought a new car. Well, it was not quite new as it had come from a friend's mother's farm. It was a baby Austin that she had used to take the chickens about with her. It was a small black car and only did about twenty miles an hour but it got us to work and back.

My job was going well and I had got a promotion. I decided that I would wait for five years before I had children because I knew my husband was not happy working as a quantity surveyor. He was bored in an office day after day. I suggested to him that we needed to make a plan for the future. We decided to make a time in the New Year to really talk.

Christmas Eve arrived and he came home with my present. He had been out with his friends and was very cheerful if not completely sozzled and insisted that I open the package straight away. As I peeled back the wrapper I saw that it was a white, orlon turtle neck sweater in a size 8 and a bottle of Primitive perfume. There was also a large block of Caramac chocolate.

I hated cheap perfume, I hated Orlon and I particularly hated turtle neck sweaters. I was also a size 12. I thought about my figure whilst eating the delicious chocolate. As I smiled sweetly my voice said "Oh thank you darling" and my brain screamed "Do you have any idea who I really am? "

THE FOURTH GENERATION

We had Christmas lunch with my parents and Christmas tea with his parents that year. As I was sitting on the sofa, surrounded by his relatives watching Morecambe and Wise, I closed my eyes. In that delicious state between sleep and wakefulness I let my mind wander. I imagined a time when we would have our own family and a beautiful house to live in, with roses round the door. I visualised a picket fence and a snowman in the garden and children's laughter tinkling in the air. I heard a sound and had to really force my attention back into the room. I was sitting between my large father-in-law and my small grandfather-in-law and they were arguing about the relative merits of the show they we watching.

CHAPTER 53
The Moon Landing

That year I used my Christmas money to buy more books. I bought *The Godfather* for Grant and for myself I bought *Travels with my Aunt* by Graham Greene and *The Edible Woman* by Margaret Attwood.

I loved reading and I knew it improved my mind. I knew I was considered boring at work because we did not have a television. There were discussions about Hadleigh, The Liver Birds and Softly Softly police show. I really had no idea what they were talking about and was sure it was time to invest in a television.

We settled into a pattern where Grant was out and about a lot in the evening and I was at home reading. Many nights I would lie awake until 3am until I heard his key in the lock. I quickly turned the light out and when he came to bed I would say sleepily" What time is it?" "Shuhhh, go back to sleep its only midnight" he would whisper.
I harboured thoughts of putting a rolling pin by the bed and whacking him like a cartoon character. I feared it would only make things worse. In January the Beatles performed that last gig on the roof of Apple records and we were all very sad.

As the year wore on several things happened at once. Grant went into Radio Rentals and ordered a television. He had been keen on space travel since he was a boy. In March he had been fascinated by the maiden supersonic flight of Concorde. He could recite the speech that President Kennedy had made in 1961 promising to land a man on the moon before the end of the decade. The date for the landing was billed July 20th 1969 and so the promise was kept.

The television meant that we could watch the space landing from start to finish in the comfort of our own home. It turned out to be very exciting but not very comfortable as lots of friends turned up and I ended up sitting on the floor!

CHAPTER 54
The Steamed-up Caravan Windows

The summer had started very sunny and we had decided to take a caravan holiday in Anglesey. It was very fortunate that we had taken food supplies as the rain started to bucket down the minute we got there.

There were only two kinds of things to do that week in the rain. One was of the talking kind and the other was of the romantic kind. The thing was that we really had not done either one or the other since we had been married. I loved him so much but did not really know how to reach him. I wished that I could talk to someone about this but I must have inherited mother's privacy gene.

We decided to have that talk we had been putting off since New Year. Grant explained to me that he needed more excitement in his life. He wanted to apply for a job that he had seen in the *Telegraph* as a rep with an oil company. The job was in Manchester and better paid so we could buy our own house.

I thought he should stay with the profession that he had studied long and hard for but he really fancied the open road and so he won me over. My last thoughts on the subject were, "I really intend to concentrate on my career and we are not going to have a family for a few years so he can always change his mind." He heard that he had got the new job a couple of days before the moon landing.

The next night he decided to visit his grandfather and left me washing the dishes. As I waved him a cheery farewell I began to feel very strange . Then without any warning I threw up in the sink. "Gosh I thought." I thought "gosh" a few more times over the next few days as I continued to be sick. I had picked up a bug in Anglesey and I decided to visit the doctor to see if he could give me something.

When the doctor saw me he asked me to stick out my tongue and prodded me about a bit. I had stopped having B12 injections the year before but still having regular check-ups. He asked me to come back in about four weeks and "Bring a sample with you." From that day on I threw up in the morning, in the afternoon and in the evening. I even threw up whilst lying in bed if I moved my eyes. I was losing weight at an alarming rate.

It was mother who suggested to me that maybe the bug I had picked up in Anglesey was maybe of the baby kind.

CHAPTER 55
The Calamine Lotion Bottle

I knew my career plans would go awry and I knew I would only be twenty years old when I gave birth but I was more delighted than I had ever been in my life. I made a promise to that little person that I would devote my life to whoever they turned out to be.

A trip to Austin Reed was in order as my husband was starting his new job. He bought a grey suit to go with his navy wedding suit. He looked so smart as he drove off in his new car. I was so proud of him that morning. I was having the day off work as I was going to the doctors with my sample.

I caused great merriment in the doctor's surgery as I could only find a large calamine lotion bottle in which to take my sample . I had rinsed it out and filled it to capacity. The nurse gently told me they did not need much and after I had seen the doctor I realised there was a lot I did not know about the pregnancy business.

I was feeling pretty fed up that evening. I had been constantly sick day and night for two months and had expected the doctor to help me. All he said in a rather patronising matter "Women have been sick for millennia, you will have to get used to it. It will pass"

When Grant came in from work I was hoping he was not expecting any tea because I could not even go in the kitchen without heaving. He stood before me with a large bunch of yellow freesias.

The smell was so intense that I clasped my hand to my mouth and whispered hoarsely." Just take them outside, please "When he came back I noticed that he had a very pale face and his hands had a faintly visible tremor. There was a bead of sweat on his forehead and I fixated on that as he spoke to me.

"I have got something to tell you," he said. "The good news is the job seems great," and then he took a deep shuddering breath," and the bad news is it's in Wales. "I think that was only one of the very few times in my life that I fainted clean away. I continued to go to work on the bus but it took me a long time to get there as I had to dismount because I felt so ill. When I arrived in the office I spent a lot of time lying on the marble floor of the executive lavatory staring at the ceiling. It never occurred to me to stay off work; I had a certificate that announced to the world that I was never absent and never late.

CHAPTER 56
You Need a Maternity Dress

The fashion was to start wearing maternity clothes at about four months into your pregnancy. Mother made me three outfits each more horrible than the last. I was dressed in garments that went down past my knees with high collars and long sleeves all because I had a little person inside me. The modern girl in the mini skirt who loved music and dancing seemed very far away.

I almost gave birth three months early with the fright I had just before I left work. I was walking back to my office when Mandy who worked the switchboard shouted and asked if I would just hold the fort while she nipped to the bathroom. I did not mind doing this as her office overlooked the front of the store and I could people watch.

It was two minutes after I sat down I took my first call. A deep, sonorous voice said "This is El Fatah; there is a bomb in your store." I felt my heart jump and I knew I had to stay composed. I knew the drill. I had to press the buttons that sent the secret signal that told the management that they had to move quickly and I had to ring the police. I pressed the buttons to dial the police station and passed the message on as succinctly as I could. As they were continuing to question me I could see that customers and staff were beginning to gather outside the store. I then gathered my things and headed down the six flights of stairs. The manager came to thank me and called me a taxi. Fortunately it was not a bomb that time, but scary none-the-less.

I never went back to my job. We had bought a house in small Welsh village with a completely unpronounceable name. I had been saving hard in the building society because that is what you had to do in those days. I had a gratuity from my employer because I was having a baby and so I could just manage the £375 that we needed for the deposit. The problem was that women could not own houses .My husband had to buy the house in his name. The fact that I thought so unfair was the first stirrings of my feminist feelings.

The house was very pretty. It was brand new, detached, and had a big garden. There was a porch, a long living, dining room and small kitchen. There were three bedrooms and a small bathroom. However there was nothing in the house but a small sink unit .There were no fittings, no heating, nothing at all.

We moved in In December but it became obvious that I could not stay there. It was snowing and we had very little furniture and no money to put heating in. My mother and mother-in-law decided that I should stay with them on alternate weeks until the baby was born. The trouble was I was a very unpopular guest. I threw up at least a dozen times a day and there was very little sympathy in 1960s Manchester. People asked around and no one had ever heard of anyone who had been sick like this.

My mother was convinced my baby would be "like a skinned rabbit," and my mother-in-law was heard to say, "you are putting it on my girl, have a dry biscuit and breathe properly."

CHAPTER 57
The Case of the Missing Baby Clothes

In the weeks before Christmas my father was invited to a reception in London. Mother always packed his suitcase for him and left it in the hall for him to pick up as he was leaving for his train. They had two black suitcases and the only difference between them was that one was old and one was new. As he rushed off for his meeting he kissed her goodbye and picked up the suitcase. Mother went back to her knitting and listening to the radio.

As the train journey wore on, he reached over head for his suitcase, a little self-importantly, and opened his case to extract his work. To his surprise when he looked down all he could see were twenty two items of baby clothing. Mother had been knitting since the day she knew she was going to be a grandmother and there was an array of vests, matinee jackets and socks in tasteful shades. Mother had packed these in tissue in the old case.

That morning she made a mistake and handed him the wrong case. He burst out laughing as did the whole carriage and he had to buy all new clothes in London. The story caused much merriment throughout the Christmas holidays that year. I enjoyed Christmas but was desperate to be in my new home and start my own family traditions. The insomnia that had haunted me from childhood continued unabated. Then I read an article by the journalist Peregrine Worsthorne in the *Sunday Telegraph* that stated "if you should be asleep then you would be asleep. "It helped me to put my sleeplessness into perspective.

CHAPTER 58
I Love Your Dimple

Those winter months dragged on for ever. I was waiting to start my life in a new decade, with a new home and best of all a new baby .It snowed very hard that winter and as I was making one of my stately journeys between mother-in-law house and mother's house I fell smartly on my bottom in the middle of the road.

I packed my small case and was dressed for the weather. My most important possession was my Dr Zhivago fur hat. I was convinced that I looked like Julie Christie from the neck up.

It was Monday morning when I waved Grant off to begin his week away. I was really glad to be going to my mother's house. Whilst appreciative of my mother-in-laws hospitality my head was spinning. Mother-in-Law Laura was one of a family of six sisters and two brothers. Her mother Alice was a really sweet woman who had died just before her 90th birthday.

She never lost the elegant air of the spinster that she had been for many years. Born in 1880 Viola lived all her life in the country with her parents and sisters and had never had a boyfriend. Her parents liked their gentile life and the daughters were not expected to marry. However it soon became obvious that something was wrong with Alice. When the penny finally dropped she was closely questioned and finally her father went looking for the handsome young man that had passed by whist building the railway.

He finally caught up with him in Nottingham. The young man was from a family of cobblers but seemed pleasant enough. His family appeared happy and persuaded him to face up to his responsibilities. A wedding was arranged in Derbyshire. The gentle woman in her late thirties who had expected to live with her parents all her life went on to have the first of her eight babies. The thoughts of the young man in his twenties on this day were not recorded.

My mother-in-law did not inherit her mother's calm nature. She had an opinion on everything and voiced it very firmly. I was constantly cheerful, always wanted to see the best in people and have a go at anything. That frankly got on her nerves. When she described somebody she liked, it was always as "she's a nice quiet girl"

Her opinion of me did not improve the day Mr Edge the milkman came to tell her that her unfailingly cheerful daughter–in–law was lying in the road. Legs akimbo, coat askew but clutching my precious fur hat I must have looked such a fright. By the time she got there some of the neighbours had got me to my feet. Once I got up and my shame subsided and I thought the show was over. However another neighbour had rung 999 and the ambulance duly arrived in the snow.

There was a conference of the ladies and it was decided I should go to hospital "as it was a pity to waste the ambulance."

I really thought the waiting was over for me as the baby was due the following week. It was not to be as I was pronounced perfectly fit. The doctor was heard to say. "Plenty of padding on that bottom, it would protect quads." My mother insisted on keeping me in after that debacle and I was driven to reading the dictionary, the Bible and back copies of my sisters Jackie magazine. I was at this point considered a hazard on the camp bed and allowed to swop places with my eight year old brother Harry.

My due date was long past when they decided to keep me in and induce my baby. Suffice to say the day was long and hard. The midwife was new, the doctor had just come out of training and I did not know what the heck I was doing. When they handed my baby boy to me I knew then that this was what I was made for, to be the best mum I could be forever and a day. He was gorgeous with black hair, dark blue eyes and a dimple in his cheek

CHAPTER 59
The Expired Roses

When Grant arrived with his mother he was waving a large bouquet of dead flowers He had bought the roses the day before and clutched them to his chest so hard during the long day and night that they were completely expired. I left him with his son whilst I went off for many stitches. I am sure I heard one of the nurses say "Wow! Forty-two and still counting."

I was going to stay with mother for a week's recovery. The following day Grant said he had to go to an important function that evening. I begged him not to go but he was insistent. His car had broken down on the way to the hospital and so he hired another one. The only one they could give him was a brand new Rover. He looked very smart in his evening jacket as he left and mother tutted as she slammed the door. "This is unacceptable," she muttered darkly.

She was muttering even more when the doorbell rang at 3am. A policeman stood there with her dazed and grazed son-in-law next to him." This young man has had a road accident and is lucky to be alive."

His explanation was long on hyperbole but short on actual facts. It seemed he had been giving someone a lift home, taken a wrong turning and ended up on an unmade stretch of motorway. The mangled Rover was perched precariously 70 feet in the air above a busy motorway. How he escaped with his life that day I do not know. The picture of the wrecked car made the *Manchester Evening News* and mother suggested it was time we went home to Wales.

CHAPTER 60
And Life Rolls on Smoothly

When I arrived back at my new home in the snow my wonderful neighbour had been in and lit the fire. As I put my gorgeous 3-day old son in his crib I wondered what the future had in store for us. Life settled into a routine and we watched the World Cup on our new television. England was knocked out by Germany. A few days later Edward Heath dislodged Harold Wilson's Labour Government. The papers speculated that Wilson only lost the election because of the World Cup defeat. Brazil went on to win the contest.

I loved that summer: the sun shone constantly and we had a lovely party for all our friends and relatives. I was so proud of my new gorgeous baby and my new home.

The only thing on my radar as the year rolled on was what happened at The Albert Hall in November. The Miss World contest was disrupted by protesters throwing flour at the stage. They were protesting at the exploitation of women.

I thought about my burgeoning opinions on women's rights. Then I remembered something. I had done a fair amount of modelling when I was seventeen and eighteen. I had modelled dresses, outfits and even swimwear and not thought twice about it. I decided then that I would always think about all the information available before giving my opinion, when more information about a subject was available then you were allowed to change your point of view.

I really hated the mantra I had grown up with "It is so because I say it's so and I know best." Who knew best? How did they know? Where did they get their information from? I promised myself I would always weigh up the information before jumping to conclusions.

I thought about this years later when I heard Margaret Thatcher's "This lady is not for turning" speech.

PART TWO

CHAPTER 61
A Dedicated Follower of Fashion

I twisted this way and that trying to fasten the waistband of the skirt I had taken into the changing room. There were two problems with the fitting. First was the struggling seven month old under my arm and second the four month baby bump that was playing havoc with my waistline.

Living in the back water of rural North Wales now meant that my uniform was trousers and a sweater. All I ever listened to was radio four and all I ever read were books to the baby. My one secret vice were gripping episodes of *Peyton Place* on the television. I loved Mia Farrows urchin haircut and wondered if I dared be so brave,

Grant had a meeting in Manchester and so had agreed that I could go with him I had a plan to have lunch with the girls from work that I had hastily arranged. I spent that morning running between the bathroom, as I was still throwing up and back to the bedroom to check out my clothes. I finally selected a pink and white dress, tasteful but still a mini dress.

On the 40-mile journey we had to stop several times but finally we arrived in Piccadilly. He helped me out of the car and put the carrycot on its wheels. He said goodbye and arranged to meet me in three hours at the same place. I was so busy fastening Theo in safely that I did not look up for a few moments. When I did finally glance up, a feeling of horror swept through me.

Here I was in my pretty pink mini dress with my pale lipstick. As far as the eye could see were fashionable city women rushing about in their very long skirts. I had been listening to radio four and enjoying radio three in the sticks. Neither station had mentioned the arrival of the maxi skirt.

My office friends knew me as someone who loved fashion and that wasn't about to change now. I looked at my watch and thought "I have just about got time" and ran like the wind into Lewis's store. Putting the baby under my arm, I left the carrycot at the bottom of the stairs and ran up three flights to Ladies Fashions. I contemplated the lift but I was petrified of them and could not risk my precious babies being stuck in one if it broke down.

I saw a skirt that might fit the bill. I rifled through for a size 14 and yanked it off the rack. As I held it up with my free hand I realised it was brown with a blue trim. I looked around for a blouse and grabbed the nearest one I could see. That was the start of the tussle in the changing room. Fortunately the assistant was really nice and took the cash to the till whilst I stuffed my discarded mini dress in my bag. When she bought my receipt I thanked her and I ran down the stairs, fastened the baby in the carry cot and hurried to the restaurant.

My friends were delighted with my gorgeous boy. I was hot, bothered and the skirt itched like mad wherever it touched my skin. I felt great though as my reputation as a follower of fashion was intact. I felt young and fancy free.

CHAPTER 62
The Chester Collapse

I met my husband and as we drove home I contemplated two things. I wondered why it had mattered so much to me to still be fashionable and why I had not been sick for the last three hours.

That really was my last rushing around day. As my pregnancy progressed I began to feel quite odd. I really had not been well since being ill in my teens. I had a lot of numbness in my legs and hands. I had also lost the vision in my left eye a few times for short periods. I had been checked out a lot during the last year because I was pregnant but of course failed to mention my symptoms.

Pregnant women were weighed, prodded and poked within an inch of their lives in the seventies. Every care was taken and ante natal classes were compulsory. In those classes you learned every aspect of baby care. Our nearest shopping centre was Chester. I really loved our trips into that beautiful city. We tried to go at least once a month but that shopping trip turned out to be different to the rest.

Grant was walking down the street pushing the pram and fortunately was holding my hand at the same time. My left leg went dead and then I went straight down on to the pavement. A helpful passer by assisted Grant and they managed to get me to the car. My baby bump was quite large by then and so I agreed to call and see the doctor on the way home. Dr. Roberts was a lovely man with small children of his own.

He saw me straight away and gave me a thorough check up. He spent ages banging my reflexes with a little hammer. He kept saying "Oh!" We went home and were just getting ready for bed when the doorbell rang. It was Dr Roberts and he had been talking to a neurologist who had agreed to see me at eight o'clock next morning. He said "it is nothing but I would like to be sure".

We spent the night talking in a desultory manner and arrived at the hospital early and the doctor gave me a thorough examination. He said "…..probably migraine, difficult to be sure". And he waved me off. As I was getting dressed behind the curtain I heard him say to the nurse "query multiple sclerosis." I have never understood why doctors and nurses think thin cotton curtains are sound proof! I decided that whatever this thing was I was going to live my life around it, in front of it and with my eyes closed. In short it was not going to get me.

My walk into the nearest town included a visit to the library where I changed the books I had borrowed for Theo. I was passionately interested in child development and was convinced that I had a little genius on my hands. I decided then that no matter how many children I had, their intellectual development was going to be as important as their physical welfare. I started to read as much as I could on how small children's brains worked and then put it into practice. I loved the *Naked Ape* by Desmond Morris.

I also tried to do some research on MS but there was not very much information anywhere. At that point in my life I realised that if I was pushing a pram I could walk nearly as fast as anyone else. I resolved to push prams for as long as I could. I had already realised that I really was not like other women. I made friends easily and enjoyed company but my mother's serious side of her personality was embedded in me and I found it hard to confide in people. I had been to a few Tupperware parties but when I was invited to a floor polish party I began to realise this was not for me. So in the weeks before my new baby arrived I spent the days playing with Theo and reading to him.

CHAPTER 63
You Definitely Cannot Watch Kojak

My brother Harry, who was about nine now spent every holiday with us as mother was working. I loved being with him and he loved his nephew, Theo. He loved me a little less when I banned him from watching episodes of Kojak. He was allowed to watch it at home but I thought it far too unsuitable. I also strongly disapproved of lollipops as I thought they could get stuck in children's throats. I had escaped all those rules from home but set myself far loftier ones that I would spend a life time obeying.

Harry was great at that time. I was feeling so ill and he amused the baby for me for hours. Harry, Theo and I were a little team.

Grant and I had completely different lives at this time. He was out early and back late and I really never went out except to take Theo for a walk. Grant was absolutely brilliant however at night. No matter how late he had gone to bed he always jumped up the minute Theo cried out. He wanted to let his pregnant wife sleep. It was one of the nicest things he ever did for me.

Theo did wake up every two hours from birth. He just could not sleep. He was awake late at night and alert before five am every morning. He was exhausting but Grant got up every morning with him and took to the paper shop to purchase his copy of the Telegraph.

On day I was in the pretty, Welsh garden with the baby. The early morning sun warmed my face but my feet were damp from the morning dew. I had woken early with a sense that my new baby would arrive that day. I had been cleaning solidly for a week and for some reason moving furniture. I had become obsessed with having clean hair and began washing it two or three times a day. That summer morning I felt beautiful, calm and serene.

My last babies' birth had been very hard work but I felt this time was going to be perfect. I was convinced I was having a girl and that it was all the oestrogen swishing around inside that made me feel so womanly. I had even had time to put my makeup on that morning. A little cold cream, then Sheer Genius for my face, pale green eye shadow on my lids and Max Factor lipstick. My hair, so very clean, had been ready to go at a moment's notice.

THE FOURTH GENERATION

At about five am I knocked on my neighbour's door and asked her to come and sit with Theo. Grant was already up and about and as I kissed my baby goodbye I wondered how he would react to the new baby. We had given a big party for his first birthday a week before but it was the only one he would have as an only child.

As we set off in our green triumph herald estate the world seemed a miraculous place. I had never been to the nursing home and as we arrived there I wondered if we had stepped back a century.

Theo had been born in a teaching hospital where everything was very clinical and cold and I had been discharged within hours. This time the paperwork from the nursing home had stated that mothers were expected to stay a full week. Dr Roberts and the Sister in charge met us at the door and within minutes Grant had been sent on his way.

I was well into labour at that time and asked if I could walk to the bathroom, I heard bells ringing and stood on a small ledge to peer out of the window. A beautiful garden surrounded the old house and there was an old gardener tending to roses and peonies. I wondered then if I really was in a dream. As I walked back midwives passed me dressed in old fashioned uniforms. The pace of life was slow and calm.

Doctor Roberts met me at the door of the room where I was going to give birth. As I lay back on the bed we were talking about Britax car seats. He had noticed that we had them in our car and said "one day every child is going to have to travel strapped in a car seat"

The next thing he said amazed me "This baby is about to be born" and in a few moments there she was. She did not cry but just gazed at me with one eyebrow raised as if to wonder who had disturbed her. My beautiful girl with a head full of auburn curls and as I looked into those startling brown eyes I felt this was the happiest day of my life.

With that she went back to sleep and a nurse brought me egg on toast. How was she to know that I only eat one egg a year and I had already had that at Easter! A few hours later as I walked around the ward I glanced in the mirror. To my surprise my hastily applied morning makeup was still immaculate. "I think I will have a dozen if they are all like this" I thought to myself with a smile.

CHAPTER 64
No One Wants to Breastfeed, Do They?

That week was remarkable for two reasons. One was that they took each baby away each night so the mother could sleep and the other was that a doctor I had not seen before made an announcement.

"Right ladies," he said to the dozen new mothers who by coincidence had all had girls. He made a jolly remark about us all either naming our girls after queens or tennis players and in the same breath said "nobody wants to breast feed do they?" With that he went round and put an injection in each bottom and our milk disappeared forever.

I arrived home with our new baby girl a week later. We had decided to call her Miranda. Friends and family visited and finally it was just the three of us at home each day. I loved being a mum. I had bought a seat to perch on top of my Silver Cross pram and we walked for miles. Miranda snuggled up under the covers and one year old Theo riding aloft chatting away.

Welsh was the language of the local shop keepers. I had studied German at school and to my ear it sounded vaguely similar. I did not understand a word of it except for "decimalisation". The first purchase I made after the currency change was pork chops from the butcher. He could speak English as well as Welsh because I had heard him. The day of the changeover he decided to conduct the proceedings in Welsh and I left his little shop convinced that I had just paid double for supper.

I had started to relax and go to a few coffee mornings so that Theo had some playmates but we were just happy being us. About a month later the baby was asleep in her carry cot in the sitting room when Theo came toddling into the kitchen. "The baby seemed hungry and so I gave her some fruit" he said. I looked at him and flew to lift Miranda up. Clenched tightly between her gums was a large black grape. I did not know whether to burst into tears or be grateful that he had learned to talk early. I smiled at him and lifted the fruit bowl out of his reach.

A month later I was feeding the baby and saw Grant's car on the drive. As I looked up he had a huge bunch of flowers in his hands.
I ran through the list, was it our anniversary, valentines, my birthday. "Oh no," I thought, "What has he done?" I put the baby to bed and as I came down the stairs he smiled at me.

"There is no easy way to say this. I hate living in the country, it is so boring. I have given my notice in and am going into business with a friend in Manchester"

It took me a moment to compute whether I was included in his plans. Once I realised that he meant all of us, I smiled weakly and said "Oh" whilst my brain was screaming "No". He set off to Manchester to start his new job and look for a house while I stayed behind to sell our house.

CHAPTER 65
The Lights Have All Gone Out

It was a difficult time for me and everyone else as there was a fuel shortage and the lights kept going out. The three-day week had been introduced to save electricity. More than once I was walking down the stairs with a baby under each arm when we were plunged into darkness. I learned to slowly sit down and shuffle the rest of the way on my bottom.

One evening when we did have electricity I decided to perm my hair. When the children had gone to bed their mother had long straight hair. About two hours later as I was admiring my curls in the mirror Miranda woke up. I had to admit it was actually a lot curlier than I had intended, well frizzy actually. As I leaned over her crib she took one look at me and started to scream. Theo came toddling in to see what the fuss was about and started to scream even louder. I could not convince my children that is was me. After a while I decided that if I could not beat them I would join them and the three of us sat on the floor crying.

I wished with all my heart that we could sell our house and we could join Grant in Manchester. My wish came true and we were able to sell our house quickly, but where were we going to live?

CHAPTER 66
Where Have All the Houses Gone?

Grant and I were standing in a queue of about 40 couples. The queue snaked up the path and around the garden of a very ordinary semi-detached house. Their embarrassed owners were standing in the hall and did not know where to look. The baby boomers were beginning to buy their own houses and there was a chronic shortage wherever you looked.

We trundled up and down the road between North Wales and Cheshire with no success. One evening Grant rang me and said, "I have seen a house. It is too big and too expensive for us but I will pick you up tomorrow about 5pm as we have an appointment to look round." I asked Dorothy next door to look after the children as we would be back late. She was the mother of five small girls and I usually had one or the other with me wherever I went and so she did not mind returning the favour.

I got dressed up for a rare evening alone with my husband and as we set off I was in high spirits. When we arrived at the house it was dark and raining. I could see the rooms lit up by lamplight and it looked very inviting.

The couple who owned the house were music teachers and moving to London. Each room they showed us looked nicer than the last in the soft lighting. There were four bedrooms and leading from the dining room was a music room with a piano. The ceilings were high and the windows were leaded. As Grant looked across at me I raised my eyebrows and gave a small nod of my head. He said to the husband, "We love the house we would like to make you an offer."
Mr Music Teacher remarked, "Up to the agent I am afraid, nothing to do with me."

With that we were out in the rain. Grant peered over the garden fence and said quietly to himself "What to do? What to do?" We ran to get back in the car and he wrote a letter of offer with the time and date on the top. The he drove to the village to put the offer through the agent's door. Finding a phone box he left a timed answerphone message of offer for the agent. "Let's hope I have some luck with the bank manager in the morning." With that he set off in the rain to drive back to Wales.

I was on tenterhooks but I need not have worried as ours was the first offer and was accepted. The bank manager was equally kind and we had a moving date for the end of February.

I had made so many friends in the two years I had been in Wales and we used that Christmas as an opportunity to have lots of celebrations. We promised to stay in touch and for a while we did.

CHAPTER 67
The Day it Rained Sideways

The day of the move dawned and the removal van arrived. The sun was shining as we left our home but as we drove towards Manchester the rain clouds gathered and the window screen wipers swished. It was still pouring as we pulled into driveway. I had a baby under each arm as I surveyed the scene. The house was beautiful but the terrible state they had left it in was unbelievable. I stood and stared in dismay, did they not know the house moving rules?

The magical lamplight had turned to dull February rain light. There was not a room that did not need cleaning and painting in that order. I checked the music room and burst out laughing as I realised the mean people had even painted round the piano. There was a room at the back of the house that looked out on the garden; it had a big bay window and inglenooks around the fireplace. We stayed up all night cleaning and decorating this room so that we would have somewhere nice to live in.

Lots of friends and family popped into see us in the next few days but the one person I really wanted to see never came. My father eventually arrived and said mother was busy but she wished us well.

My two little helpers and I decorated and sang to hearts content. Miranda sat in her high chair and Theo helped me decorate. There was a lovely garden and we planted gourds and beans and sweet peas. The first day I was there I found that the mean people had taken up every daffodil bulb in the garden and then forgotten to take them with them. "Oh Blast," I thought as the children and I put them all back in again.

CHAPTER 68
The Yellow Morning Room

I discovered that I had an eye for design and putting great looks together on a small budget. I painted the morning room yellow because the sun streamed in there in the morning. I grew flowers that summer and decorated the house with them. A cat got caught in the sweet pea net and I had to ask my father to come and rescue it for me. I bought an old gramophone and started to play the records I liked The Carpenters, Neil Diamond and David Bowie.

During this time my marriage was in serious trouble. I hardly saw Grant and when he did come home it was very late. We argued in hushed voices when the children were in bed. I hardly recognised him as the husband and father he had been before he had started working with this friend.

The only time we had put on a united front was for the guests at the children's christening party. That day was one of the few times my mother visited us. My father told me she thought she had enough to do with work and her home and did not have time to do other things.

Grant was usually out all weekend but this particular Saturday he arrived home in the early afternoon. I was playing in the garden with the children when I looked up to see a large bunch of flowers hovering above my face. Although I could not bear to hear what was coming my brain slowed enough to register yellow roses, cream lilies and white gypsophillia. The scent hit me like a blow to the head and I reeled backwards whilst trying to get to my feet.

I asked him to look after the children whilst I got some lemonade and as I returned to the garden they were all laughing. I looked at him and my heart filled with love and I thought whatever it was I could not bear to lose him.

When we sat down he reached across for my hand and said "I know I have been horrible this year but I want to make it up to you." I have stopped working with Blake and I have a job working for another oil company. The job is in the Lake District and I start on Monday.

CHAPTER 69
The Pink Magnolia Tree

I looked up at my beautiful house with my magnolia tree in the garden. I looked at the lovely brickwork and windows and thought people work all their life for a house like this. Here I am at twenty two years old and about to leave it behind. Two things crossed my mind that day. One was whether I should stay here and try and make it on my own, but I dismissed it in a heartbeat. The other thing that crossed my mind that day was whether I would ever live in such a beautiful house again.

Eight months to the day after we had arrived in that he was gone. Up to the Lake District to start his new job and find us a house. I was to stay where I was and put the house up for sale.

My sister Gillian was a student at Manchester University and still living at home. She offered to come and stay with me whilst Grant was living in The Lake District.

She was so trendy but all she ate were apples no matter how I tried to persuade her to eat. She went everywhere in hot pants. She was still dating the boy she had met at her 14th. Birthday party, but things were not going well.

They broke up and on her first night out with friends she met a music publisher in his twenties. Mother was very keen on him and I liked him too. However Gillian was in love with the love of her life and eventually ended it with the music man. My children adored her and she was great with them and I enjoyed that time. Life was just settling into a peaceful rhythm when a couple made an offer on the house.

Grant then announced that he had put a deposit down on a bungalow in Kendal that would not be ready for nine months. He had however found us a three story rental house overlooking Lake Windermere and he thought I would love it. He came to collect us the following Saturday. He was right I did love the "upside down" house from where I could see the mountains across the Lake. It was however totally unsuitable for two toddlers. There were about 10 steps up to the front door which led to a small hall, bathroom and two bedrooms. Then there was an open staircase than led up to a huge room that included an American style kitchen. Plate glass windows filled a whole wall that led out to through doors onto a balcony with a thirty feet drop to the Lake.

We were free to move in that day. I did not know what to say. It felt like a ski lodge, lovely to be in for a week, but I was going to have to be on my guard every single minute.

As dusk was falling we drove back past the large hole in the ground that was to be my bungalow. I could not change the plan to buy it as the builder had wanted stage payments and the first one had already been paid.

"Oh drat," I thought as we whizzed back down the M6. I really wished I had someone to talk to about this. I was however obeying the rules I had set for myself and bore it all stoically.

CHAPTER 70
Raleigh Choppers and all That

We moved into our picturesque home for the next nine months just before Christmas. My brother Harry came with us for the holidays and he had great fun whizzing along on his space hopper. His present from his parents was a Raleigh chopper, but really needed lessons on how to ride it. His feet only just touched the ground and like most kids he spent as much time falling off it as he did sitting on it.

The New Year started and the children and I had a wonderful time. Reading, drawing and making collages in the morning and long walks by the Lake in the afternoon were the order of the day. Painting was very popular, especially of the family of ducks that lived under the bedroom window. One day Miranda and I were watching the ducks from the window and she dropped her fat painting brush onto the grass. A second later the mother duck had picked it up and run away with all her ducklings following. Miranda was still chuckling about that a week later. We were surrounded by fields and a stream and we collected fat tadpoles in jam jars and furry catkins and yellow tipped pussy willows to put in the vases with the daffodils we bought.

I bought a twin push chair for our walks. It must have been a Friday as they were allowed Quavers on that day. There was nobody around the water's edge but us. I heard a noise and then it went dark. Seagulls swept down to pinch the Quavers. I really wanted to cry but instead I laughed and then so did the children. I thought I had child proofed the whole place but Theo was very determined. I had to watch like a hawk because if I took my eyes off them they were hatching some plan to escape.

We had a lovely time that spring and I thought "I am really happy". My marriage was back on track and Gavin was home for tea most nights and was able to put the children to bed. I was twenty-three years old. I was reading one evening on the balcony and Grant was listening to Elton John on the record player. The children were asleep and we were having a leisurely evening after supper.

I suddenly had the most terrible pain in my stomach and began to wail. I have always had the ability to override physical symptoms with my mind but I knew this was bad. I had been having twinges for a while but the doctor had said he thought they were nothing serious. I began to shake violently and Grant had the presence of mind to dial 999. I spent the time we waited gritting my teeth with the pain and begging him not to leave my children even if it meant he never went back to work again. I had a feeling I might not come back and wanted him to understand that what I was saying was critical.

The ambulance men arrived quickly and after wrapping me in a blanket tried to manoeuvre me down the open staircase and then down the steep steps to the road. Grant had no idea where they were taking me. "Kendal" they shouted as they drove off. The poor man did not know what to do. We did not know anyone in the area who could help. He fastened the balcony door, woke Theo and Miranda out of their slumber and put them in their car seats.

He drove as fast as he could with the babies in the car and turned at the first hospital sign. He pulled up into the car park, grabbed the children out of their seats and ran breathlessly through the entrance. The poor nurse on reception had no idea what he was babbling about. By that time both the children were crying. It was finally explained to him that he was in the geriatric hospital and the A & E he wanted was a few miles away.

When he finally got to the hospital they were preparing me for surgery as I had a burst ovarian cyst and peritonitis. Of course one of my self-inflicted rules were you must suffer silently and it was not the last time it would get me in trouble. I was in hospital for a while and true to his word Grant never left the children's side. The man he worked for was wonderful and gave him a month off work.

The elderly doctor who came to see me when I got home looked Grant in the eye and said "This young woman is not to have a baby in the next year under any circumstances".

"Gosh," I thought, and I was just beginning to think that would be a lovely idea.

CHAPTER 71
Gillian Goes To Italy

I really hoped that mother would take some time out to come and look after me but she never offered. My sister Gillian who had just finished her teacher training course came for a week before she left for Italy to meet her boyfriend Malcolm. I was so grateful to her and was very sad when she left. She had worked so hard to put herself through university doing two jobs whilst studying. I hoped she was going to have an amazing time.

Gillian came back to England three months later and announced that she and Malcolm were getting married in two months. There was no reason for the rush; she just wanted to be married. Mother went into a tailspin. She had a dress to make and a reception to organise. Miranda was to be her bridesmaid and Theo her page boy.

Gillian's wedding day dawned clear and bright. Well it did until she opened the curtains. It was raining sideways and stayed like that most of the day. To top it off it was foggy but when I saw my sister the sun came out. She was a perfect bride in her amazing dress. Mother had surpassed herself again. Her ability to glance at a magazine page and create an exact copy was phenomenal. Gillian looked a picture in her long white dress with its flowing sleeves. Her long dark hair was held in place by flowers and matched the simplicity of her dress.

I took a picture of my family that day and it is imprinted in my mind. We were in my parents beautiful garden under the frothy green Robina tree. Mother and Father stood smiling arm in arm. Mother looked amazing in her green brocade outfit topped by the mink coat and hat that her grandmother had left to her. Father had on his best navy suit and wide red tie with his dark hair touching his collar in a nod to modernity. The bride stood just to the side of them, gorgeous holding her bouquet of lilies that she made to match the design of mother's bouquet.

Three-year old Theo was holding his Dad's hand. He was dressed in a denim outfit with a denim cap and looked like a mini Jimmy Osmond. My handsome husband Grant stood with his long hair and kipper tie and thirteen year old Harry with his even longer hair. I smiled at them before I clicked the shutter. Where was Miranda?

I could hear her laughing but could not see her. Then I realised that she was peeping out from between my parent's knees. As everyone realised that they collapsed into giggles and I took the photograph with my heart. The wedding went beautifully and was remembered by all and included the fact that the group did not show up. It did not matter a jot as we were all in such a good mood that we sang the night away.

CHAPTER 72
I Really Need To Expand My Mind

I surveyed our new garden in the hazy autumn sunshine. I have always loved this time of year with the welcome sight of the changing leaves as you round a corner and the slightly acrid smell of wood smoke floating in the air. Autumn for me is purple michlemas daisies, pink dahlias, and bronze chrysanthemums. Lots of lovely chores to do, cutting back the plants and trees so that they survive the cold winter in safety. The best job of all in my opinion is kneeling to plant daffodils, tulips and hyacinth bulbs to welcome spring. I have always felt deep in my heart that being so close to the earth is somehow life affirming. The day I looked out of the window was very different. There was brown, damp soil as far as the eye could see.

Living by the lake had been magical whilst it was quiet and still. As spring and then summer arrived so did the tourists and it became very hard to get the car out of the drive or get served in a shop. So when the time came to move to our bungalow I was ready to go and start our new life.

We had been living there about a week on the evening that I surveyed the mud in my wellington boots. Thoughts swirled around in my brain. I knew there was only one answer and I had about week to make it happen before it went really cold. I knew my children would need to play. The builder had fenced the garden but there was not a tree to climb or a lawn to play on. In the garage was a spade, a rake and a spirit level. All I needed was grass seed.

The next day when Grant went to work I put Theo and Miranda in the twin pushchair and set off to walk the mile to town. With my grass seed purchased I put the bags under the push chair and in and around the children. What I could not fit in and on them I put in some carry bags.

It was a good job the journey home was downhill. We flew home with the autumn leaves swirling around us and the wind at our backs singing loudly all the way.

CHAPTER 73
Look At Our New Lawn

The three of us wrapped in our anoraks proceeded to dig, rake and riddle to our hearts content. The thing they loved the most though was flinging the seed in all corners of the garden. Each day we peered through the rainy window and two weeks later we were rewarded by the sight of a perfect, green swathe. They clapped and squealed with delight and I was convinced that they were going to grow up to love gardening as much as I did

We purchased a large white object that lived in the kitchen. It was all the rage, an industrial size freezer. The problem was that you could not fill it whatever you did. No matter how many peas we shelled, carrots we blanched or cakes we baked there was still room and room was the enemy. Dangerous levels of electricity could be consumed if the thing was not filled to capacity.

The trendy thing to do was buy a half a pig or a sheep and pack it carefully in striped plastic bags. We were always prepared in case anyone ever had a pork chop emergency.

Ice cream, packs of twelve mousses, arctic roll and orange lollies were purchased in industrial quantities. If there was still room left you filled it with bread. Cheap white sliced if you were feeling short of money or Blackpool milk roll and floury baps if you were in the money.

The trouble was everything was packed so tightly it was impossible to find anything you wanted also Arthur the goldfish lived on top of the freezer. I was often to be found in Booths Emporium thinking "Oh blow it, I will buy some fish for tonight."

Three things stopped me venturing into the chest freezer. I made my own brown bread, I did not like frostbite and I felt really guilty swishing Arthur the goldfish about in his bowl. When I was not cooking, baking and gardening I was playing with small children. Word got out that I was good with children and some mornings I would be found with a dozen children leaning over rolls of lining paper. I bought this in packs of twelve from the rather grand wallpaper shop on the high street. The brushes came from the ironmongers and the paint from the toyshop.

We also made modelling clay with flour and water. You had to remember to put lots of salt in it otherwise the finished article could begin to smell horrible after a few days. Afternoons were for educational visits. Into town to the museum with its frightening old bear rearing up on his hind legs. We also took the bus or the train to visit places of interest further afield.

I also resumed my education at this time as I was determined to get to teachers training college when my children were older. Each evening found me immersed in school books. Wilfred Owen war poems thrilled and broke my heart at the same time. I had always had pacifist leanings and these poems were a revelation to me. Wilfred Owen said, "All a poet can do today is warn. That is why the true poet must be truthful." His poems ignited my love of poetry that years of grammar school education never managed. I also fell in love with the novels of Thomas Hardy. *Tess of the D'Urbervilles* touched me most. The rest of the world passed around me, above me and behind me and I really did not notice much at that time. Harry came to stay and I noticed his hair was longer and he was wearing patterned shirts and tank tops. We watched a bit more television when he was with us. He loved Happy Days, Hawaii Five O and The Six Million Dollar Man. The children were allowed to watch The Waltons and The Partridge Family and my secret pleasure was he Rockford Files.

CHAPTER 74
I Need to put More effort into My Marriage

I do not really remember much about Grant at that time. I always kissed him goodbye at the front door when he went to work. The girls across the road told me I was very lucky to have such a handsome husband. He looked so smart whatever he wore but sometimes I looked at him in his navy suit and trendy wide tie and thought I should make more effort. Our relationship was cool as he was busy, I was preoccupied and there were to be no more babies for a while.

On his twenty-seventh birthday I spent the day cooking. Miranda and I changed into our long dresses and Theo had on his best outfit when we answered the door to him. I had laid the table with candles and flowers. We had a lovely meal and after we had put the children to bed we shared a bottle of wine. It was the first time we had talked in ages.

Not long after that, I was dusting the window ledge in the sitting room. I looked up to see Grant's car in the drive. With a sinking feeling in my stomach I saw that he was carrying a large bunch of peach and cream roses and gypsophillia. My conscious mind went through the tick list, birthday, valentine, and anniversary. Whatever was the matter? "Can we talk," he said

We went through his office which was at the front of the house. "I will just make a cup of tea," I said. Whilst I was waiting for the kettle to boil I slowly put a load of whites in my brand new washing machine. I picked up the tea and then went back to feed Arthur.

CHAPTER 75
And it Danced Across the Kitchen

I made myself as comfortable as I could on the plastic bright orange kitchen chair that he used for ancillary seating in his office. He sat on the plush swivel chair that matched his desk and swung round to face me. He began to explain that he was feeling trapped and never had any money for anything nice. My eyebrows shot up alarmingly.

The look on my face must have disconcerted him and he rushed on to say that all he wanted to do was move to a smaller house so we would have more money for holidays and other fun things. I was arranging my mouth to shout "No" very loudly when the house started to shake and there was a terrible crashing and banging noise from the kitchen. The children were in the playroom and I ran to get them and dashed out into the garden. I peered through the kitchen window and what a sight greeted me.

My brand new top of the range washing machine had danced right across the kitchen. Not only that but it had actually had the temerity to set on fire. Grant whilst jumping up and down was shouting "the bolt has sheared off" and "ring the fire brigade" in equal measure.

I ran next door and banged on a startled Judith's door. She took the children and dialled 999. Her husband who was home at the time remarked to her that I gave an excellent impersonation of Corporal Jones from Dads Army shouting "Don't panic, don't panic!"

Five minutes after I ran back to my house the fire brigade arrived and were putting the fire out. Our kitchen was awful and took me a week to clean. I was really put out by Judith's husband's remark and was determined to mention it to him the next time I saw him. Two weeks later I was looking after Judith's toddler James as she had gone into labour.

THE FOURTH GENERATION

The next time I saw Judith's husband was when I opened the door. He was shouting, "Help, Help the kitchen's on fire." His arm was quite red and he was holding it in the air. His face was all black and his glasses were steamed up. Two neighbours were chatting outside and they ran to take all the children as I ran to call the fire brigade. I then charged round to help, carrying my emergency burn spray that had just been invented. I insisted on spraying him quickly before joining him throwing water at the sausages.

The perplexed firemen arrived and soon put the fire out and gave us both a stern lecture on the danger of taking your eyes of sausages. He spent the next week visiting his wife and I spent the next week cleaning his kitchen as his arm was too burned to risk it. Pat across the road came to help me. A week later, when his wife and baby girl were safely home and none the wiser, he came round to say thank you.

I smiled and my voice said, "It's no trouble I am glad you are fine now." My mind thought "cheeky beggar, I bet you were glad of Corporal Jones that day and a bunch of flowers might have been nice"

The exploding washing machine had put paid to our conversation that day and it was never resumed. When a For Sale sign outside our home appeared it seemed churlish to argue with him. I was more interested in getting into teachers training college. I did however insist that the time had come for us to buy a house in joint names.

The world was changing for women at the end of 1974.

CHAPTER 76
The Small House

We found a smaller house nearby which was just about big enough for us and I convinced myself that less housework would be a good thing. I got my place at college and put my dreams of more children on the back burner.

Grant and I had become closer since the financial pressure was off him and we were having fun for the first time in ages. One morning I settled the children in front of the television to watch playschool.

I made a cup of tea and turned to wash the breakfast dishes .To my complete astonishment I was sick right there, in the sink. "Hello" I thought. I did not need a doctor, a test or anything else to tell me I was pregnant. I ran into the garden overcome with joy. A baby, another baby. What could be more marvellous? I had yelled so loudly that Pauline my new neighbour peered over the hedge. I was lying on the grass and beaming from ear to ear. She said "What are you doing?" and I said" Yoga."

My mother and Father came to babysit as we were going to an annual company dance. They still lived about eighty miles away in Manchester. As they came through the door Theo and Miranda could not contain themselves. I was standing in the kitchen in my tiny house in my very long, very glamorous evening dress. It was pale green, the same colour as my face as I was still throwing up at least a dozen times a day.

My four year old son said "Granny I really, really want a puppy" and my three year old daughter said, "I really, really want a baby and we are getting one!" Mother peered around the kitchen door, took one look at my pale face and said, "So, it's true then."

"We made it to the dance in Harrogate with only four stops. I was OK until the food arrived. Large sides of roast pork with twinkly sparklers sticking out of them, big tureens of mashed potato and the strong scent of boiled cabbage filled the air. I looked at all these elegant women in their finery and wondered how there were going to dance after eating this lot. Then I clasped my hand over my mouth and ran for the door.

Our hotel room was on the first floor and I spent the evening lying on the bathroom floor in my pale green dress. I had a pillow over my head trying to block out the hits of Abba, David Essex, Mud, John Denver, Suzi Quatro, Osmans, NewSeekers. I convinced myself if I ever felt well again I would never, ever be forced to listen to "Waterloo" again.

I had not seen much of mother since we moved to the Lakes but I had seen a lot of my father. He loved the area and always stayed with us when he was travelling north on union business. His union was a white collar union led by Clive Jenkins and the unions were beginning to become very powerful.

I knew mother loved her house, her job and her garden and really did not like spending even a night away. That was why I was dumfounded when they arrived unannounced one afternoon. Mother had a bunch of fragrant, blue hyacinths in her hand. I was delighted to see them and gave them a big hug. As I turned to run the water for the flowers and the tea kettle I took a deep breath. "What is the matter,?" I said with trepidation they never visited unannounced? Mother had had an operation for stomach ulcers the year before and she was still very thin. A tendril of fear wound around my heart.

In my anxious state I could not compute what father was saying "……..near you. We are coming to live in Kendal….I am opening an office of the union here….."My sister Gillian had been in Italy for a while after graduating. She was now married and living with her husband in a flat in central Manchester. My brother Harry was fourteen years old and loved his life. He was an avid Manchester United supporter and very independent.

I smiled and ran to hug them and my voice said "Great news it will be wonderful having you near" My brain whispered "Can this be what she really wants? When I got her alone I asked her the question. My serious private mother smiled a very tight lipped smile and whispered "It will be alright."

Our new house was at the end of a cul-de-sac and there was only one way in and one way out. If I had taken the time to think about that, I would have realised I found this extremely claustrophobic. However I did not have time to listen to my thoughts then. I was feeling really ill. The numbness and the dizziness were back and I was throwing up ten or twelve times a day. I also had Theo and Miranda with who I was determined to keep my promise to do my very best. There were days when they painted and played and I watched them whilst heaving over a very large bowl.

One morning I just could not get out of bed. As much as I tried to move nothing happened. Grant was busy and as he was rushing out of the door I burst into tears. He rang the doctor and as he sat on the end of the bed I thought he looked so very out of place in this domestic scene. I heard Dr Land's footsteps on the stairs. I was glad it was him as he was my favourite. He was young, calm, kind and plain spoken. He stood in the doorway surveying the scene and his eyes rested on Grant. "This girl is very poorly and either you do more around here or she is going into hospital until the baby arrives." He placed his hand on my forehead and said darkly" I will be back here tomorrow".

I knew then that the only time I was going to stop being sick was the moment I gave birth. It had happened with Theo and Miranda and would happen with this little boy. I was convinced that the baby was a boy. I had been right both times before and so I had only bought blue baby clothes. We decided to call him either Julian or James and we would wait to see him to decide.

I knew they were building a lovely new house at the end of the cul-de-sac. I could see it from my window and I watched the progress with interest. One day father arrived and I could tell he had something important to say. "We have sold our house and bought one here in town." I loved the fact that they were coming to live close by and hoped to be able to really connect with mother. However I reeled at his next pronouncement.

"We have bought the house at the end of the cul de sac but it will not be ready for two months. I start my new job on Monday and I am not leaving mother behind. We will just have to stay with you for a few weeks. The next week mother and father moved into our bedroom and Harry had a camp bed in Theo's room.

This was a small house compared to all the other places we had lived in. New houses were built with one long thin living room with a dining space at the end.

The rest of my pregnancy was spent sleeping on a double camp bed in the dining space. I never even asked myself "Why?" My parents were only in their forties, but making sure that they were comfortable was important in my house.

CHAPTER 77
The Day finally Arrives

The weather was lovely as spring turned to summer and I spent most of my time in the garden with the children. Mother was not happy and spent most of the time reading. I asked her if I could do anything but she replied "I just feel exhausted." I worried about her and brought her another cup of tea.

Moving day finally arrived and they walked the 100 yards to their new home to wait for the removal men. We had agreed I would keep the children out of the way and when the van drove off we walked across. It was lovely, light and airy and their furniture fitted beautifully. I looked at her face and she looked so unhappy, my heart went out to her.

Phone lines were a precious commodity and they had been told they would have to wait six months for a phone. I agreed they could have a party line with us. The only down side to that was that you could not ring the other party.

My due date was only days away and I thought a walk would do us good. I put on the only dress that still fitted me, a blue gingham peasant dress, that mother had made for me. It flowed away from my body and kept me cool. Putting sun lotion and hats on Theo and Miranda we set off to visit Granny and see if she wanted to come with us. The children were very excited by the prospect of mother living nearby. I knocked on the door and it took ages for her to answer. The kitchen curtains were still closed and I smiled and invited her to come with us. "No thank you," was all she said as she disappeared back into the stygian gloom.

My parents-in-law arrived the next day and took the children out for the day. I had woken up feeling as though the baby would come that day but had not mentioned it to them. When Grant set off for work I said "I am in early labour, please keep in touch. Will you also tell mother on your way out to work?" I stood in my dressing gown and watched him stop at her house and go inside. He was on his way two minutes later.

I had had a difficult labour first time and then a very easy labour second time. As I made myself a pot of coffee I felt very happy. I had made an assumption that each labour got easier so it was going to be a breeze. Mother could not ring me, because of the party line but I assumed she would be over any time soon.

I decided to take a shower. I preferred a bath but there was too much danger of getting my enormous frame trapped. I used my new Opium shower gel and washed my hair so it would look nice next day when I returned home with my new baby. I had insisted that I only wanted to stay in the nursing home for one night as I did not want to be away from the little ones.

I checked my bag and picked up a magazine and went to sit in the chair by the window. I could look out for mother from there as I was convinced she would be arriving soon.

As I opened *Good Housekeeping* I took a sip of coffee and glanced out of the window. I could see my mother on her knees on the gravel facing her front door. I started in alarm, was she ill?

Then things slowly began to fall into place. A few days ago she had showed me a box containing tiny mosaic tiles. She had a hatred of concrete front door steps as she had whitened so many in her time. She intended, when she had a free day, to mosaic the front door step

Well today was obviously a free day because she was tiling the step! As the temperature soared and my labour pains became more and more intense she knelt, like a penitent in front of that door. Hour after hour she carried on placing those tiny mosaic tiles, never looking up. Hour after hour I sat, lay and finally knelt on all fours visualising the baby boy who was making his way into the world.

It was going dark when Grant came back from his meeting. My mother-in-law had decided to stay at her daughter's house for the night and Theo and Miranda were safe with her.

CHAPTER 78
He is a Long Way Off Dear

We finally arrived at the nursing home and I congratulated myself on leaving it to the last minute. I was admitted and the midwife, who was a neighbour, came to greet me. Sister Lea was everything you would want in a midwife. She was round, pink and had a mop of white curls. She seemed utterly capable and composed. She examined me and then sent for another midwife. The consensus was that this was a large baby that was not ready to be born. I smiled and nodded even though by that time I had been in labour about 14 hours.

This was the first time that Grant was able to be with me for the birth, because fashion had changed in the early seventies. A father's attendance had gone from being frowned upon to becoming almost obligatory in a few short years. The night wore on, the labour was more difficult and I looked at Grant. I burst out laughing. Here I was, unable to move freely because of the machines and drips that were tying me down and gripped by the tumultuous waves of my baby's journey into life. There he was, in a tee shirt and jeans, chewing the mints he had bought for me and reading the sports page with interest. We were both going to have a new baby by morning.

The night wore on and Grant read out cross word clues to me and a newer, much meaner sister arrived. There was a little incident at three am when after examination she announced "The baby is a long way off, yet" By that time I really had enough. I complained very loudly and the sister said to me "Will you please calm down, you are frightening the young mothers. "I looked at her mean face through hooded lids and thought "I am only twenty five years old". I pursed my lips and did not say another word.

The morning wore on and Sister Lea came back on duty. As she walked in the room I realised Dr Land was behind her. I heard him say, "Let's get this baby out of there." Minutes later they handed me my ten-pound boy. Bright blue eyes, a shock of black hair in a quiff and my heart melted.

I looked around for Grant and could not see him. I looked out of the window and saw his back disappearing into the distance. I knew then that this would be the last baby I would ever have. My joy was undimmed by a series of events that happened that week.

I heard a bit of a kerfuffle in the doorway, there was a baby missing from the nursery. I saw the look on the matron's face as she walked towards me and hysteria rose like bile in my throat. I do not remember much else. Minutes later a young health visitor came running in with James in her arms. He was soaking wet and wrapped in a towel. There was a simple explanation. Sarah was running an ante natal clinic in the building next door. She had decided to take my baby for "show and tell" as he was the biggest baby and had lots of hair that she could wash.

Against all the rules she had forgotten to mention this to anyone. She burst into tears as she dropped him into my arms. My voice said, "Don't worry, don't worry. He's ok, and I am ok." My brain was screaming "You stupid woman, you almost stopped my heart." I was so looking forward to going home but a problem arose.

I asked a nurse that was bringing me a cup of tea if she could straighten my pillows. This turned into straightening my covers and as she lifted the sheets I heard her say "Oh, my goodness" and she ran off. Dr Land was in the building and he came running. Within minutes they brought in a contraption and although my body was on the bed my legs were high above me attached to this metal support.

It was explained to me that I was covered in big red spots and that meant I had phlebitis and they had to prevent it from getting worse. I was going to be in hospital for a while. Grant arrived that evening. As I was trying to explain to him I had phlebi......he thought I said I had said fleas... and ran to complain to anyone that would listen about the standard of hygiene.

Mother came to see me and my son on the third day. Grant had taken a week's holiday and so the other children were fine but I could go back only wave to them from the window.

CHAPTER 79
I Need my Medicine

Finally our little family left together to go back home and I thanked the staff as they had been excellent. It was only as I looked back to wave goodbye that I realised not one person had brought me a bunch of flowers.

A few weeks later Theo was due to go back to school. He had done a term from Easter to summer and was one of the youngest in his class. He was a kind, caring little boy and was doing really well. He could read long before he started school and appeared to be really good at maths. He had had the summer at home with his family and the new baby and I could see he really did not want to go back to school. We talked about it and as he left me that morning he seemed quite cheerful and glad to see his friends.

As I was preparing lunch I heard a knock at the door. It was the head teacher holding my little boy's hand." I have brought him for his medicine," she said. "Medicine, what medicine?" - "The medicine he must have before lunch otherwise he will become very ill." He had explained his illness to Miss Maud his teacher and she had taken him to the headmistress.

As we stood talking in the kitchen we both realised that this little boy had been so desperate to get home that he had concocted a plan of escape. We both raised our eyebrows and then looked down at his little dark head that was busy studying his shoes. Fortunately she was a kindly, sensible woman and said, "I think he better stay at home for the rest of the day. I am sure he will be better tomorrow."

I have always been a very poor sleeper and in the long, dark hours a thought that I had been pushing down in the day came into my mind. My Father was a very determined man whose opinions had dominated his children's lives. He also thought he dominated his wife but I was really not so sure. I made a promise to myself that as a mother of three, I was not going to be swayed by father's view of the world.

It was tradition in our world that you never disobeyed your parents no matter how old you were. Then when you got married you started to call your husband's parents mother and father. I thought at the time that it was a way of proving dominance over the interloper in the family.

Harold Wilson had won both the 1974 elections for the Labour party. One of his election pledges was a referendum on the UK membership of the European Economic Community. Ted Heath had been the Conservative leader who had taken us into Europe in 1973. Heath was an elegant man who loved classical music and sailing. He was also a passionate Europhile. That was one of the first times I remember hearing Margaret Thatcher's name. That promise I made to myself disappeared when father asked me to help with the European Market "No" vote campaign that year. I spent a month helping with the campaign. I was talking to people on the doorstep, putting leaflets in envelopes and making tea at meetings.

When the result was announced it was 52.1% yes and 47.9% no. We gathered at the Labour party to hear the result and as the crowd dispersed they wondered about what might have been if they had got a few more voters out. I wondered why I felt so relieved; it was of course because I thought we should stay in Europe.

Not for the first time I wondered why as a grown women I was still programmed to do what her father instructed her to do. My father was really happy in his new role and spent his time being very busy and important. He was leader of the local labour party and insisted that we should all go to the meetings, He organised lots of speakers and I met Tony Blair and Ken Livingstone as well as lots of other labour MPs. Father's best friend was a labour MP and we thought that he may stand at the next election. Mother was more socialist in her views but declined most invitations because of her deafness.

CHAPTER 80
Mother's Beanie Hat

I was walking through the town one day pushing James in the pram and chatting away with my little girl. Miranda loved life and was always jumping and skipping and chuckling. She had almost perfect recall and was reading well even though she was not due to start school for six months. I saw my parents on the other side of the road. Looking at them as an observer I realised just how detached they had become from each other.

Father was walking in front with his head held high, smart in a navy suit and the red tie he always affected. He was smiling and nodding at people as he passed them. Mother was walking about four steps behind. She had on a long grey coat and what could only be described as a beanie hat. She was also dragging a shopping trolley behind her. She was looking at the floor and did not speak to anyone.

I went into the local Italian coffee shop and ordered cappuccino for me and ice-cream for Miranda. As I was sitting there I wondered what I could do to help my parents. I decided to go into the lovely

THE FOURTH GENERATION

store across the road and buy my daughter a new winter coat. My interest in fashion for myself had disappeared but my one real vice in life was to buy beautiful clothes for my daughter. The coat was absolutely divine. Royal blue velvet with cream toggle buttons it had a sheepskin lining. Then there was the pale blue smocked dress that I had found to go under it. The purchase had made a big dent in my housekeeping but we skipped all the way home.

I tried not to worry too much about mother as she, father and Harry were going on an extended trip to Vancouver to see her sisters. I had finally passed my driving test and agreed to take them to the airport. Harry did not want to go and he sulked all the way there as only teenagers can. I had offered to let him stay with us but mother had insisted. As we stood waiting for the plane I asked mother if she was looking forward to her trip. She looked me and said, not for the first time, "I don't do excitement."

Grant had taken the day off to look after the children. As I drove back along the M6 I felt a soaring sense of freedom. I put the Carpenters tape on the cassette player and my foot down. I was in my mid-twenties and had a handsome husband and three gorgeous children. I was going to enjoy the next few years.

CHAPTER 81
The Good Life and the Prawns

I decided to concentrate on the garden. I wanted to grow vegetables, lots and lots of vegetables. Whether it was the influence of the BBC television programme "The Good Life" or the health of our growing family I did not know. We bought a greenhouse and started planting seeds. The garden at the side of the house had been deemed ideal and Grant had taken up the lawn and dug the whole thing over. I had added the fertiliser and raked it until it was perfectly friable. The children loved it being out in the fresh air.

Miranda was doing well at school and both she and Theo enjoyed their days there. Miss Grant knew I was interested in child development and asked me if I would be interested in spending two hours on a Monday morning listening to some of the children read. I broached the subject with mother to ask if she would mind having James for a couple of hours at the start of the week. To my amazement she agreed and I started the following Monday. I absolutely loved it and renewed my commitment to myself to train as a teacher one day.

When I picked my growing baby boy up two weeks later she met me at the door with a frown." Monday morning is not convenient for me as I like to do my housework early, you cannot go again" and that was that.

I loved being with this blonde little boy and he looked so cute in his pram in the shade of the apple tree. We spent hours in the garden but I had to remember to put on sun lotion as the weather was becoming very warm indeed.

CHAPTER 82
The Year of the Drought

1976 was a year of change in Great Britain. The sun shone and everyone seemed to be enjoying life. That summer felt endless with the songs of Abba everywhere. It soon became obvious that we were heading for a massive drought. Nationally the Prime Minister appointed a minister for drought, Dennis Howell.

Water restrictions were everywhere and lots of people depended on stand pipes for their supply. Grant had an idea to set up a water shoot from the bathroom window to the vegetable patch. Although Action Man enjoyed his water slide again and again, the dreadful mess the contraption made in the bathroom made him eventually give up. We realised that we would have to let our vegetables wither on the vine. We heard the stories of people sunbathing in the park and men frying eggs on the pavement.

I was running a bath for the children one evening and realised I could see little prawn type creatures wriggling around in the water. I rang a friend whose husband worked at the research centre on the shores of Lake Windermere. The problem was that what was coming through the taps was from the bottom of the reservoir and the little

THE FOURTH GENERATION

creatures were part of that sludge. The children, of course, did not want to get in the water.

When Grant came home he told them the story of the disappearing villages and promised to take them at the weekend. When the City of Manchester needed more water for its growing population in the early half of the 20th century, some Westmorland villages had been flooded under the new reservoirs. The villages had reappeared in the drought and were a real tourist attraction. The children had a lovely day and we stopped at The Swan in Newby Bridge for lunch.

A smartly dressed lady in the restaurant came up to us and said "What beautiful children you have, they are so well behaved .They are such a credit to you."

I was really glad that she had left the place twenty minutes later. We were sitting at a low round table. Theo and Miranda had slowly been moving the table around inch by inch. I could see they were up to mischief by their giggling. I did not know what it was until the table tipped off its axis and complete mayhem ensued.

1976 was a year of strikes and inflation. As well as being a national officer for his Union, father was also responsible for negotiating his colleagues pay and conditions. He got into conflict with the bosses and eventually called all the officers out on strike and it made the national press. Father was high on power and mother was devastated that his story and salary had been in the paper for the entire world to read about. The shame of her family knowing how much her husband earned was almost too much for her to bear.

There was economic failure in the country and the government was forced to ask for a bale out of millions of dollars. Inflation raged at 17%.The heat affected the population and riots broke out at the Notting Hill Carnival. Music had a complete about face that year. It started with Abba and Elton John and a feel good factor. It ended with punk rock, the Sex pistols and the Clash

It started raining in October Dennis Howell became Minister for the Flood.

CHAPTER 83
Give Some of your Christmas Money Away

We had a new baby in the family. My sister Gillian had a girl Claire as the year drew to a close. My father, mother and I drove the eighty miles to see the new family. My sister and her husband Malcolm were still living in their student flat .The baby was gorgeous and the plan was to leave mother there for a few days. Father and I drove home in silence as there was a pea soup fog and we were both concentrating. As he dropped me off, he said, "I bet I will be back there in the morning" and of course he was.

The year drew to a close with all the lovely things that happen when you have small children. I was now on the PTA at the children's school so helped organise the Christmas fair. We had decided to make Christmas a time of family, fun and lovely food. I abhorred the commercialism that was emerging and liked the children to have one big present and a lovely stocking. I firmly believed that birthdays were the time for lots of presents as there is no such thing as too much birthday.

Mother also insisted the children give to others at this time of year. We all gave some of our Christmas money to mother's favourite charity. When I saw Gillian at Christmas I could see that she was just wiped out. " Please help me find a job for Malcolm up here. I really need to come and live near you and Mother "I promised her that I would make that my New Year's plan

Just after Christmas we received a call from some dear friends who were in town. She was ebullient and charming. He was just the opposite, quiet and reserved. They had emigrated to America where he had created an amazing invention to do with plastic. They loved their life in America and intended to stay but the dollars had started to mount up so they had returned on a flying visit to find a holiday home in the Lakes. We arranged to meet at the elegant waterside hotel where they were staying. It had a world class restaurant and we were really forward to the evening. I had cut my hair very short and wore a cream trousers suit.

When I saw Mollie I admired her outfit. She had on a silk blouse that matched a long skirt that fell to the floor. We always had fun when we were with them and this evening was no different. The only thing I noticed apart from the delicious food was that Mollie was knocking it back at twice the rate the rest of us were. Gerald kept giving her the evil eye. She eventually excused herself to go to the powder room as she delicately put it, gave her five minutes and then followed her to see if she was alright. When I eventually caught up with her I nearly fainted. She was chatting away at the front desk in her Texas/Cumbrian drawl. There was nothing wrong with that picture except that after going to the loo she had very carefully tucked the back of her beautiful silk pleated skirt into her rather small knickers.

"What can I do, what can I do,?" I thought. Then without missing a beat I walked straight up to her and put my arms around her waist. As she carried on chatting to the startled maître D I began to unravel the voluminous skirt out of her pants. When she finished her conversation she put her cheek against mine and said, "I do miss you," and walked back to her seat none the wiser.

CHAPTER 84
The Queen has a Jubilee

This year was the Queen's Silver Jubilee and everyone was making plans for celebration. The Queen embarked on a series of appearances. She managed to cover more of Britain in just three months than any other sovereign.

She made official visits to the commonwealth including Canada, Australia, New Zealand and the West Indies. In early June the Queen lit a bonfire at Windsor and travelled in the State Gold Coach to St Paul's Cathedral. Everyone loved it, everyone except my mother that is who thought it was a "lot of tosh".

It came as no surprise when the Labour government revealed that inflation had put prices up by 70% within the last 3 years. We did not realise that inflation was such a bad thing. Father always said, "Inflation means the working man can afford a washing machine." I thought, "Yes, that's true as long as he gets an above inflation pay rise."

My sister had moved to be near us in the spring. Gillian, Malcolm and Claire stayed with mother for a while and then found a house about two minutes' walk away. Some days it was lovely having my mother, father, brother and sister living so close by but other times it was suffocating.

Everyone's life has its ups and downs and most of the day to day things are better kept to you. When you have words with your partner in the morning you have forgotten why you were so cross by teatime. I spent some of that precious family time worrying about stuff that was really not important. I felt as though I had no choice as I was in charge of making people happy. Our little family life was really good at this point. Miranda and Theo were enjoying school and had lots of other activities going on each evening.

We were members of the local Methodist church and the children went to Sunday school every week. The Sunday school teachers were amazing and worked so hard to make sure the children had fun. James was baptised there with all the small children around him. Mother kindly knitted him the most delicate all in one turquoise filigree outfit. The trouble was that he was eleven months old and walking when we finally got round to it. The large baby had grown into large toddler with shoulders like a line backer.

I knew I was going to upset someone and so I chose my mother over my son. Mother would have been upset if he had not worn the outfit and James was going to be really upset when he saw the photographs. I never collected the offending photos and they may still be collecting dust in the chemist on the high street for all I know.

CHAPTER 85
We Need a Bigger House

One day Grant came bouncing in and said "Come on we are going to look at a house". With our growing family we really were stretched to capacity in our small house. The house he had found was only fifteen minutes away from where we lived. He said to me "our lives will remain the same, we will just have more room".

THE FOURTH GENERATION

I dreaded telling mother we were moving and I had no idea why. She was unhappy from the moment the idea was broached. We discovered that the new house would be ready in about four months and we were confident we could sell our house as we had enjoyed living there.

We did sell it quickly and that created a problem. There was a week gap between the very last day the purchasers needed to move and our date of completion. I called round to see her and gently eased the conversation around to the subject of the new house "Would it be alright with you if we came to stay for a week before we move". She fixed me with her cool green eyed gaze and said "Absolutely not!" There was a deathly silence and I said "Why ever not? "They had stayed with us so many times over the years. She gazed at me again "I really don't want the bother." I shrugged my shoulders and left.

We had heard about Forestry Commission Cabins and so I rang to see if they had a vacancy anywhere. Cornwall "was the answer and so I booked it on the spot. Grant thought I was unreasonable not to have said something to her. "Go and argue with your mother," he said.

Mother had built a wall around herself that was as high as the sky. She had always had strong views about politics and religion and since moving north she had become much more introverted.

Whilst she was working she had friends and a reason for being. She once said to me "You never laugh with your family like you do with your friends at work". She was too busy reading about the serious stuff in the world to think about mundane domestic trivia. There was not much room for laughter in her life at that time.

Society had changed dramatically in the 1970s. The baby boomer generation were subservient to their parents and then they became subservient to their children. The generation born after the war were the vehicles of change. They became the parents who regarded their children as amazing creatures for whom no sacrifice was too great, but mostly their parents had regarded them as something to be endured.

I loved Katherine Whitehorn in the Observer. Her quotes were legendary. "Never make sacrifices for your children as they will not appreciate it," She also said. "I am all for people having their heart in the right place, but the right place for a heart is not inside the head" I wondered if she was right then decided she probably was wrong in the first instance but right in the second.

CHAPTER 86
Cornwall for Five Days

The next week we packed our belongings and put them in storage and set off to drive the 800 mile round trip or 5 days. We loved the Forestry commission properties. Set in areas of natural outstanding beauty they were all over the country. Looe was beautiful that week. The cabin was deep in the forest. The wildlife was amazing, woodland that was home to red deer and only 15 minutes from the coast.

When we got the key and entered the cabin I saw something that I had not seen before, a triple bunk. I hardly slept a wink worrying about Theo who had chosen the top bunk. We dined on fresh mackerel from the fisherman on the quay and took several boat trips. We called in a café and asked for five cream teas. The waitress burst out laughing and said. "Two will be plenty between five of you."

Of course she was right. Two cream teas filled the table and we all staggered away replete. The thing the children remembered for years though was the endless games of table tennis.

When we got back from Cornwall we collected the keys for our new house from the agent. Although I had enjoyed the holiday I was still feeling very cross with my mother. Maybe it was a sign that I was finally growing up. I can honestly say I had never felt this way before. That night I looked at my sleeping 3, 7 and 8 year old children huddled together on a camp bed and thought "what's wrong with this picture".

The next morning I realised there was water running down the walls because the plaster was so wet? I ran my fingers over the steamed up window and noticed that father had thrown all my greenhouse plants on the front garden.

We moved into a hotel that night until the walls had dried. I never, ever knew what Mother's objection to us moving was.

I promised myself that when the children were older and they had anything wonderful I was going to celebrate by whooping around the kitchen... I have kept that promise.

Theo joined the cubs and Grant opted to run the football team. He had never really played football but had watched enough of it in his time to have a good idea. His motivation for offering to do this was to make sure Theo got a game. He was determined to make sure that all the boys got a game and this did not go down well with some of the more competitive dads.

Miranda was a keen ballerina at this time. When her lesson had finished we always went downstairs for an ice-cream at the Italian café that was underneath the ballet studio. Then we went to collect the boys from football. The football field was in the windiest part of town. I really did not mind washing all the kit week in and week out. However, I really resented the parents that arrived late to pick their kids up because, well, suffice to say their excuses were myriad and mostly rubbish.

The Brewery Arts Centre became very important in my life at that time as I was looking after James and my sister's daughter Claire. Gillian had gone back to work and as I was at home anyway it seemed sensible to look after both children together. The Brewery was excellent as the children could learn to do anything there. Most courses were offered in the thriving theatre, music centre and arts departments there was a small playgroup at the Brewery and after a few weeks I started to get involved in fund raising.

CHAPTER 87
Let's Jump in at The Deep End

My motto has always been "Lets jump in at the deep end and see what happens" I organised a gala evening at the Town Hall. There was a fashion show, music, dance and a raffle. All went well until the dance group called in sick. I persuaded Miranda to fill in with ballet routine that she had performed for about a dozen parents a week before.

She was a trouper and agreed to my request. The look on her face as she whizzed around the stage in front of 150 people, dancing with a teddy bear, was something to behold. She still gets a faraway look in her eye if ballet is mentioned.

That year Elvis Presley died. This was an excuse for Grant to play his records loudly in tribute to the King He was always convinced I that I loved Elvis as much as he did. It was many years later in Las Vegas whilst watching an Elvis impersonator that I decided to tell him I actually preferred Cliff.

Our new next door neighbours were very sweet. They were both social workers with two little boys about James' age. I often babysat for them as they had no family in the area. The father Eddie had a shock of red hair and was quite a bit older than Gill the mother. She soon tired of not working and got a job at the hospital as the duty social worker. The first weekend that Eddie was left to supervise the family Connor the toddler, overdosed on indigestion tablets and needed a visit to casualty to be checked out. The second weekend dad was not looking and Connor decided to give himself a shave and needed a return visit to the hospital. On the third weekend Eddie decided to keep the children together and built a model aeroplane. The result was that Connor super glued part of the model and his fingers to his face. Another emergency room visit ensued and the doctor decided to call for the social worker. Poor Gill was red faced with shame when she realised it was her family and resigned on the spot. She was laughing through her red hot tears as she relayed the story to me.

CHAPTER 88
The Women's Room

Leo and Miranda were at school and I was in the library with 4 year old James. He had found the books he wanted and I was gazing lazily along the rows of feminist literature to see if anything caught my eye. I still had my mother's penchant for serious books. Like her I believed that romance novels were a waste of time.

However unlike her though, I did love a good mystery novel. During my sleepless nights I worked my way through the works of

Raymond Chandler, Agatha Christie and Dick Francis. During this point of my life I was searching for something different and feminism had caught my attention. I still longed to live in America and the stories of the fascinating women captured my imagination. I could not read enough about Gloria Steinem, Andrea Dworkin and Germaine Greer.

The book I found that day changed the whole course of the next phase of my life. I had not worked for nine years as I believed that the children needed my attention. They had all stayed at home with me until starting school and I had concentrated absolutely on them. I loved little people and watching how their minds developed day after day. Conversations with a three year old that made you fall about laughing. How you needed to get down to their level to get the full meaning of what they were saying.

One evening I was peeling the potatoes for tea when I heard a little boy say, "Mum ……the human race." - "What about the human race darling, it is a term that means all the people in the world?" He stamped his foot, "No mum it doesn't." I put the peeler down and looked at the child. He stood there and looked at me, from behind him peered a small white dog. "Mum, I said I am having a dog and human race."

That evening when the children were in bed I began to read *The Women's Room* by Marilyn French. *The Women's room* is set in 1950s America and follows the fortunes of Mira Ward a traditional and even submissive young woman in a traditional marriage. She makes friends with other women in her neighbourhood. Natalie, Bliss and Adele. They are all like her married with children. The story follows her gradual feminist awakening.

Mira and her husband Norm move to a small town and she makes friends with Samantha, Martha and Lily and lives through the pain and heartache of their lives. Eventually, after her husband files for divorce, Mira goes to Harvard to study for a Phd in English literature.

The book follows the lives of Mira and her friends and ends with her teaching in a small college alone. When the book was published in 1977 it was criticised by some feminists for being too pessimistic. I read the whole book in one sitting and realised it had crystallised a fear I had in the bottom reaches of my heart.

CHAPTER 89
I Definitely Need a Job

I had been married since I was a teenager and although I adored my husband I was not sure my life would be plain sailing. On the plus side I knew my husband was kind and loved his children deeply. On the minus side I knew he was reckless, impulsive and craved excitement and as I lay in bed that night that I knew I needed a job.

The reason I gave to everyone that asked was that we needed another income if we were to have the nice things in life. Only I knew what my real reason was and I was not about to share that with anyone.

We had booked a gîte holiday in Normandy and we were to go away at the start of the school holidays. James was to start school in September and I thought it would take me a while to find a job. I grabbed the local gazette as it landed on the mat. As I moved my cup of tea I smoothed it out on the table and turned to help wanted. There was a large advert for the Tax Office which had its office half a mile from my home. I rang for an interview and was given an appointment the next week.

I rang to see if I could get James in the local nursery for the few months before he went to school. The headmistress of the nursery was lovely and assured me there was a place. The day of the interview I looked at myself in the mirror and thought that I looked like a different woman to the one that had left work a decade ago. I imagined that tax work was very dry and boring but the main thing that would make it work for me was that they offered flexi time.

The interview went well and they offered me a job. When I spoke about flexi time there was a silence. The manager really did not like it and so they had stopped offering it to new employees. As my heart sank the girl who showed me out whispered" They offer flexi time at the DHSS down stairs, why don't you try there"

CHAPTER 90
Excuse Me, Do You Do Flexitime?

So I did try and they did offer flexi time. I needed another interview and some of the questions startled me. What did I think about Princess Margaret? I could tell him what mother thought about Princess Margaret. I did not think that answer would go down very well. I mumbled something about her being a nice woman and it must have been the right answer as I was offered the job there and then I was to start on May 5th 1979.

I got a lot of strange looks when I told people I was starting work. I was known as a mother that was really interested in her children and people could not understand why I had made this about face.

I worked and worked on my plan. Everyone had to be in the right place at the right time. There could be no distraction or deviation from the master plan.

The plan was pinned to the wall of the breakfast room and by and large it worked. I went in the office early whilst Grant took the children to school and I got home early and he worked late. My sister Gillian who lived nearby had stopped work to have her second baby and she was a great help.

About a month after I started work I was just exhausted by working and doing all the housework. One Saturday morning I went to spend half an hour in my private space, my greenhouse. The simple act of opening the door and being assailed by the powerful scent of the tomatoes and orchids entranced and calmed me.

Miranda had gone to ballet with her friend. Her friend's mother and I took it in turns to take our daughters every other Saturday. Grant had taken the boys swimming and so I had a little time for gardening. As I stood in the greenhouse I closed my eyes and drifted off into a reverie. The next thing I heard were gentle sobs and I realised they were coming from deep inside me opened my eyes and the sobs got louder and louder. I was surprised that I was crying but tucked away corner of my mind I knew that I was really enjoying the experience.

I stood and cried and cried and eventually the door slid open. Grants voice said, "Whatever has happened here?" I fell into his arms and clung onto him like a life raft. Finally when the tears had subsided and I said, "I am so tired." When he realised that all I wanted was for him to help more around the house he complied in a heartbeat.

Mrs Thatcher won the election a few days after I started work. There was a rumour round the office that her first act would be to cull the Civil Service but that seemed to fizzle out. My mother hated her with a passion and always referred to her as TBW (That bloody woman).

Mother was still very political at that point and spent more hours than ever reading the *Guardian*, listening to the news and following current events. She also took *Private Eye* and *The Economist*. Mother had been a very attractive woman but would no longer let me perm or colour her hair. She let it go grey, had it cut short and affected the style of the academic that she really should have been.

CHAPTER 91
The Gîtes in The Forest

That summer we had our first summer holiday abroad. We had decided to stay in a gîte near Rennes. As we set off in our Morris Marina we whooped with glee. The good news was that it was a brand new company car. The bad news was that it had a sloping back and so all our luggage had to be squashed in...

We completed the 4-hour journey in record time and arrived in Weymouth to witness the big tractors sweeping the sand. We boarded the ferry without incident and found seats by the window. The children loved the 4 hour crossing to France and were delighted as we disembarked at Cherbourg.

We were in a foreign country and Daddy was driving on the wrong side of the road. We felt very relieved when the garage accepted our European cheque and felt we could relax. Grant and I both had French O levels but we had bought tapes for the journey. The "How to learn French quickly" tapes were soon put away as the voices were making us fall asleep.

THE FOURTH GENERATION

The gîte we were expecting turned out to be a log cabin in a forest. We realised quickly that this was going to be a good thing as we could see families sitting outside their cabins. As we pulled up a French family came to greet us. They offered to give the children a snack as we unpacked. We said, "*Merci*" and they went to sit outside next doors log cabin. Grant unpacked whilst I stood peering round the door jamb in case my babies were suddenly in danger.

They came back absolutely full of stories about their 30 minute adventure. The lady had given them chocolate on baguettes and a peppermint cordial to drink and they played swing ball with the children. I feigned great surprise at all this news. Of course I already knew this as I had been watching every move they made. That evening as I put the children to bed I heard the "pop" of a bottle of wine being opened.

As we watched the sun go down, Grant turned to me and said, "I think we are all going to enjoy this holiday "We certainly did enjoy every single day. Theo, Miranda and James played tennis, swam in the lake and made lots of friends. We browsed the local shops for good things to eat and were invited to a different family's bar-b-que every night. Grant was particularly pleased with the quality of the local wine.

I put aside my feelings of embarrassment at my appearance on the day we went to Paris. I was absolutely covered in psoriasis. Head to foot, no exception that could only be covered by a long black dress, black tights and makeup for sensitive skin. I had had spells like this throughout my life and they could go as quick as they came.

Paris was all I had dreamed of and was worth the 600 mile round trip. The children enjoyed lunch in a real restaurant and fell about laughing at the antics of the French drivers. They all double parked and if someone was in their way they just physically bounced the offending car up and down until it moved.

It was in the early hours of the next morning that we finally arrived back at our holiday retreat. As Grant carried the sleeping children to bed I looked around for the painting I had chosen with such care on the Left Bank of the Seine. I was still laughing when Grant came back.

Rubbing his hands He said, "So show me our painting then." - "I would love to," I said, "But somebody left it on the roof of the car as we drove off". The whole holiday was perfect and we kept in touch with friends both French and English for a long time.

We were determined that the journey home would not spoil our memories of the trip. The ferry was late because the English Customs and Excise were working to rule. That meant they were emptying every car and checking its contents. We disembarked thinking we were on our way but worse was yet to come. We sat on the dock for 14 hours. Fortunately we had never been known to go on a journey without emergency supplies. We were lucky we had food and drink and we shared this with the families around us. The children were excellent as they had books to read but it was very boring.

A loud bell went off at one point and everybody around us jumped. There was an investigation and the source of the terrible clatter turned out to be me. I had put my large Westclock alarm clock inside the pressure cooker that I took everywhere with me. The alarm clock had gone off, fallen sideways and was loud to enough to frighten the whole docks.

When we finally reached customs we could see harassed fathers shoving all their possessions back into their cars. The same fate befell us and they took everything out of our car. The only thing they confiscated were Miranda large pine cones that she had so carefully collected. We had never seen ones so large and we would never see them again as they were carried off in a box as though they were a ticking bomb.

CHAPTER 92
The Year I did Three Things …

My little brother got married. Harry and his bride had a registry office wedding and in the weeks before I made the cake and iced it in a very elaborate style. I thought it was marvellous but the photos we saw later told a different story. It looked like the leaning tower of Pisa.

THE FOURTH GENERATION

I spent the day before the wedding arranging the flowers. I was in heaven because the scent of the roses and lilies filled my senses. I was in hell because I felt Harry was far too young and should be finishing his education. Big fat teardrops landed on the bouquets and button holes.

I spent the actual ceremony holding my sister's week-old son. As I clasped him to my chest more big fat teardrops fell on his soft little cheeks. Harry looked so young and vulnerable as he recited his vows. I really liked his wife but it was all too soon.

Grant was furious with me by the end of the day. I had spent so much time staring at the baby and weeping that I had taken my eyes off my 4 year old son James. He had gone around the tables in the restaurant finishing off everyone's champagne and had to be walked around and around the car park until he was less wobbly. I felt very old that evening. The week previously I was driving passed my sister's house.

Her kitchen window was at the front of the house and I waved to her as I went by. I drove to the next corner and stopped. Some thing was very wrong. I will never know whether I saw or felt the problem. I turned the car round and screeched to a halt outside her house. When she saw me she came outside. She was pregnant and the baby was due in a month's time. The problem was that she was twice as big as she had been the day before when I had seen her. Her face was like a balloon all tight and distended. I asked her if she was feeling ok. She said, "not really, we have been Christmas shopping all day in Manchester".

I asked her where her daughter was and she told me she was with her Dad watching television. I popped my head round the door and told him I was just popping to the doctors with Gillian. I said quietly "Malcolm how could you not have noticed that your wife is so swollen now compared to how she was this morning"

I helped her in the car and hurried to the doctors. He took one look at her and called the ambulance. Of course, she had preeclampsia and it was well into the night before we knew she and the baby were going to be Ok. I felt very old that night as well.

In December I went to a gig at the University with my friends from work to see The Stray Cats and Squeeze.

I had been a few weeks before to see Dave Edmonds and Nick Lowe and I thought "I could get to like this." I danced and danced until I could dance no more. I felt very young that night. I was 29 years old.

CHAPTER 93
My Cookery Book Collection

I have always been a passionate collector of cookery books. I have scoured book shops, antique shops and flea markets. I am always grateful for a cookery book as a gift for birthdays or Christmas. I actually very rarely follow recipes but just love to hold them and read them when I cannot sleep at night. I have all my mother's cookery books. Her favourites were Mary Berry and Marguerite Patton. My two favourite books are ones that I have had for a long time. I bought Jane Grigson's *Good Things* in 1973. The picture of the eggs on the front entranced me. I still love to read it particularly as it mentions my uncle's Suttons Kipper Fillets as being world famous.

The other book I cherish actually changed the way I cooked. *French Provincial Cooking* by Elizabeth David was first published in 1962. Elizabeth David was a British cookery writer who changed British cooking with her articles about European cuisine. I tried her pot roasts, ragus and carbonnades. I loved her omelettes and potato gratin.

Slowly the hotpots and stews of my youth were replaced by these delicious dishes. I still made my own bread, yoghurt jams and enough lemon curd for every fete and show in town. I have no idea why I kept doing this. I only know it gave me the same feeling as I got when I opened the greenhouse door first thing on a warm summers day. My family loved my new recipes and the only complaint I had was that I cooked far too much of it.

CHAPTER 94
My Own Unbreakable Rules

If a guest knocks on the door you WILL invite them in with a smile.

If a guest comes in, you MUST offer them a drink and preferably a homemade cake or biscuit.

If a guest stays a while, then you have a DUTY to invite them to stay for lunch or supper.

If a guest has a long journey ahead then you MUST offer them a bed for the night.

When the guest sets out on that journey you MUST make them a packed lunch. This packed lunch MUST include sandwiches, crisps fruit and a preferably homemade cake. Whether or not they got a drink depended on their answer to this question. "Are you stopping for petrol?" If the answer was negative then they would get lemonade or a flask of coffee. If the answer was positive they were invited to buy their own drinks at the garage.

As my children got older that rule was extended to their friends. There was very rarely a time when there was just the five of us at home. Even when our children were well into their twenties we could have a houseful of American Students or French students. I have absolutely no idea where that rule came from; I just knew it had to be obeyed.

CHAPTER 95
I Can Rule The World

As a new decade began I felt that I could rule the world. Theo, Miranda and James were all doing well at school. They were at that wonderful stage of life when there are interested in the family. They smile, eat the meals you prepare and happily accompanying you on family outings.

Grant had bought me a smart blue mini. My life was filled with trips to school and work. I also whizzed to cubs, guides, scouts, judo guitar lessons, chess lessons, ballet, football, tennis and all the stuff I was convinced would expand my very smart children's minds.

THE FOURTH GENERATION

I was really enjoying my job. It involved meeting people and I loved everything about it. Even though the job was clerical in nature I had been asked to sign the Official Secrets Act and that made me feel very grown up.

It was a revelation to me that people listened to your opinion, you could go to the loo in peace and best of all they paid you as a present for turning up. I tried hard to make sure I was dressed smartly even though I dressed with my eyes closed each morning because I was so tired. One morning it was lunch time before I nipped to the ladies. As I washed my hands I gazed at my reflection in the mirror. Across the left shoulder of my pink sweater was a red and white checked tea towel.

Over the years I had developed a of habit of flicking a tea towel across my shoulder as I whizzed about the kitchen. I just had forgotten to take it off that day.

When I got back to my seat I asked Sue who sat next to me why she had not told me about my fashion faux pas. She shrugged and remarked, "I just thought it was an artfully placed scarf." I thought then about all the women who went out to work after doing a full day's work before 8 am.

My theatre director sister-in-law was working as a dinner lady to fit in with family life. She always cycled to work, rain or shine. The independent school she worked at was rather smart and had a long winding drive. As she dismounted she fell to one side and wondered if she had had a stroke. She looked down and realised that she had one very high heel on her left foot and one completely flat shoe on her right"

My friend Val had rung me recently with a tale of woe. She had found a new job in a solicitor's office and had been warned that lateness was frowned upon. As she jumped out of the shower that morning she was busy putting little peoples arms into their clothes. She opened a new packet of   knickers with her teeth and struggled her damp body into them with one hand. She rushed into her office, sat down and began to realise that she had a terrible pain in her nether regions. As she sat there the pain got worse and worse and began to wonder what had finally "gone" after four difficult births. She rang the doctor and her saw her straight away. As he straightened his high velocity lamp for a better view he was overcome with laughter as he extracted the offending sticky label.

CHAPTER 96
The Slow Cooker, The Microwave, and the Dishwasher

Grant was true to his word and did everything I asked. In fact the point was that I did not have to ask, he just knew instinctively what had to be done and then did it. He fitted a beautiful new kitchen and we had a dishwasher and a microwave for the first time. Every morning, as well as getting everyone ready, I prepared the evening meal and threw it in the slow cooker.

The ballet that was our lives at that point was the same no matter whether Mum or Dad played the music. My quandary was that I had to go on a course in Newcastle. I asked Grant whether he would be alright if I was away for four days.

He assured me that he would and the family took me to Carlisle to get the train to Newcastle. I had been booked into a boarding house run by Mrs Peacock. An amazing cook with a tennis playing son she made me very welcome. The office was only two minutes' walk away and so the visit was perfect.

It would have been except for the fact that I had not realised that I would have to share a room. This was the Civil Service in 1980 and saving money was everything. Amanda, from North Wales, was lovely. Sleeping was still an elusive state for me. As I padded back down the corridor a voice rang out "Anthony, Anthony, and Anthony". I looked across and her breathing was still regular, she was still asleep shouting Anthony, Anthony Anthony."

I never discovered who Anthony was or what he was doing but I do know he did it all night every night for three nights.

CHAPTER 97
They Are off To Cuba

Mother seemed to take on a renewed vigour at the start of the 1980s. Father wanted to travel and she eventually agreed to go with him. It was lovely to see her coming back off holiday relaxed. She had a list of places she wanted to visit starting with Cuba and ending with St Petersburg.

The visit to Cuba was the first to be arranged. In those days you were not allowed to fly straight to Havana from a British Airport. You had to fly to Ireland first. We took them to the airport and they were in great spirits. They flew from Manchester into Shannon Airport.

The wait there was arduous because they had to stand 12 hours in a queue. Mother said that they were surrounded by Russian tourists with their possessions in cardboard boxes all shouting at each other.
Their first impression of Cuba was of the cheeriness of the people but also the poverty and the heat. When they got to baggage reclaim father's case was nowhere to be seen and it remained stubbornly missing for the rest of the holiday. That was the least of his problems though.

When he went to buy some more clothes he discovered that the average Cuban man had a 30 inch waist. His waist, even when he breathed in his hardest, was at least 40 inches. He spent the whole fortnight in the clothes he had travelled in. Mother was desperately rinsing them through each night and leaving them on the balcony to dry.

Well she rinsed them through for the first week and then she slipped and twisted her ankle. Fortunately she had brought with her the emergency crepe bandage, so all was not lost. When she looked in her first aid kit she was devastated to discover that her precious possession was gone. It had been replaced by an ordinary bandage by her careless daughter- in –law.

She spent the whole week trying to find the Spanish word for crepe bandage. It appeared not to exist in Cuba. There was also a complication on the boat trip which included lunch. Although they both had a smattering of French, the native language of Cuba appeared to escape them. They misunderstood the instructions for

THE FOURTH GENERATION

lunch and actually ate the fishing bait thinking it was a very poor Cuban idea of lunch. They were highly embarrassed when a sumptuous spread arrived but by then they were not hungry.

They were tanned and relaxed by the time they came back. The idea of Cuba was more exciting that the reality as I think they had imagined Fidel Castro would meet them at the airport! In the same way I was so disappointed that Tom Selleck was not waiting for me, with lei to place around my neck, when I arrived in Hawaii.

Television has a lot to answer for!

CHAPTER 98
Swot Shop Versus Tiswas

As our children grew more interested in the outside world we started to watch more television. We watched the first showing of a Bond film *Live and let Die* as a family.

The children loved Swap Shop and it was getting harder to get them out of their pyjamas on a Saturday morning. I preferred Swap Shop to Tiswas as I considered it to be less anarchic!

When Theo was not playing his Pacman video game he was trying to solve his Rubiks cube. He did not need much sleep. After the the others were in bed he would come down and we would put the world to rights. He had really interesting opinions and I really enjoyed his company.

Miranda loved her *Girls World*. It actually freaked me out a bit I had to admit as it was a disembodied head on a stand. She put makeup on it and did its hair to her hearts content. It actually came to a sticky end when her brothers accidently landed on it whilst wrestling.

James loved anything to do with Star Wars. I had no problem with the Millennium Falcon but I hated the At-At figure with a passion. It looked like a metal dog and its eyes followed you everywhere. As I tidied the toys up in the evening I could not bear to touch that thing. If it was on the floor whilst I was ironing I had to carefully move behind the sofa with my foot.

CHAPTER 99
We're Going to Tenerife Without the Kids

As I signed the permission slip for Miranda to go on a brownie's camping trip, a plan was forming in my mind. Theo who was 11 yrs. old desperately wanted to spend a week in Manchester. He enjoyed his friends who lived next door to his paternal grandma. We had known the family who lived next door to my mother-in-law for ever. Gladys, the mother of the family was lovely and one of her daughters had been my sister Gillian's best friend at school. Jean was now a doctor in London. The two youngest brothers were as different as chalk and cheese. The younger boy at 11 was quiet and academic like his sisters, the older boy at 12 was more outgoing and there was a definite look in his eye. They also owned a large Great Dane. I did not worry though as I knew my mother-in-law would be very strict.

I dreamed of sunshine and fun that day as I stood with the slip of paper in my hand. I decided there and then to go and ask mother if she would look after 5 year old James for a week. I found her in a good mood that morning and she heartily agreed that a break would be good for me. I gave her a hug and then hastily left before she changed her mind.

I had lost a lot of weight since I had started work and had recently realised that I had hip bones to go with my newly acquired cheek bones. My psoriasis had completely disappeared with my growing confidence.

A day later I had sorted a plan out for half term for my children, booked a holiday and bought a bikini. Tenerife here we come.

CHAPTER 100
The Lush Green Gardens

Our plane journey was uneventful. I had never flown before but I actually loved the sensation. I felt very anxious leaving my children but once I was on my way I was determined to enjoy every minute. The heat hit us like a brick wall as we left the airport at

Santa Cruz. We were on the north side of the island as we had been told it was a little cooler and prettier than the south.

The gardens of the hotel assaulted my senses. There was an old man watering his carefully attended verdant space. Bougainvillea in shades of pink and purple covered every available wall. The plants of an English garden were well in attendance, roses, lilies and sweet peas were everywhere. My mother's favourite plant strelitzia reginae stood to attention everywhere. She loved the bird of paradise flower and had made several attempts to grow it from seed. I truly knew then the meaning of the word lush. I have the image of that garden stored firmly in my mind. It is still the place I go to if I need to escape for a moment to centre myself.

I was so enjoying myself that I hardly noticed the room they showed us. It was lovely and as I peeled back the curtain I was delighted that I could see the garden in all its glory. The evening meal was part of the package and so we headed to the restaurant expectantly that evening. The food they offered us was inedible. Grant took me by the hand and said" Come on let's find a nice restaurant"

The dreadful food in the hotel seemed at first to be bad luck. We decided however that it was our good fortune because it meant that we tried every restaurant in town. Flambéed bananas, sizzling prawns, fish casserole with potatoes and the mojos sauces were all new to us and tasted divine.

We had been told the beaches were black volcanic ash and so after a tourist visit we decided to stay by the pool. I enjoyed the feel of the sun on my newly beautiful skin and relaxed. When I opened one eye and peered at Grant from under my hat I could see he had a very sad face. I could tell that the sound of children playing in the pool was like a knife in his heart and he really missed his children so much.

We had a wonderful time but we were both glad when it was time to go home. As I looked at my son when I collected him from his grandma's house I could see he had grown in height and in confidence. That little taste of freedom had been good for him. I knew I fussed too much but I could not help my nature.

I thanked my mother-in-law and youngest sister-in-law and gave them a necklace each that I had bought on plane for them. Theo was full of stories about walks to the river with the boys and games of cards with his Grandma long after his normal bedtime and the journey up the M6 was over in a flash.

We collected Miranda from the friend whose mother had picked her up from the coach. She had had a lovely time with her friends even though she did not care for brown owl who she regarded as "very bossy". I actually agreed with her as Betty the Brown Owl was a single lady never met your gaze, she just barked orders to an area round about bosom height. Luckily Tawny Owl was very nice. She was mother to lots of daughters of her own. Miranda looked relaxed and I thought a little taste of freedom is a good thing.

When I saw James he just raised his eyebrow at me and carried on drawing. It was like a little stab in the heart. I thanked my mother and sister and gave them the necklaces I had bought on the plane.
Within a short time we were home and my little boy had given me a big cuddle. I looked around and thought how lucky I was. I had enjoyed my delicious taste of freedom too but I would not be going on holiday without my children again.

CHAPTER 101
My Child has gone to Heidelberg

Theo went on his first school trip that summer. He went to Germany and I packed lots of different things for him to eat in his case as I knew he was a bit fussy. I was in two minds whether to let him go as he had started with allergies earlier in the year and had developed asthma.

I had done some research about allergies earlier in my life because Miranda had developed some kind of allergy when she was about 4 yrs. old. Her swollen lip had come up on Mothering Sunday and we wondered if was handling daffodils or primroses that was the cause. The doctors frankly did not have a clue about allergies in those days and it was put down to "one of those things".

THE FOURTH GENERATION

Research meant going to the library and reading books that had been written long ago or trying to engage experts in conversation. I read as much as I could about the subject and decided to make a diary. For three months I wrote a diary about everything Theo did. The weather, where we went and what we ate all went into the little blue book. I knew he hated fuss and so I tried to do it all surreptitiously.

I then concocted a diet that I thought might work. I talked to the doctor about it. He said "You are a sensible women, I am sure it will be Ok"

We all shared that diet on the basis that it would be good for all of us. By and large everyone went along with it. The exception was the goat's milk. I found a farmer who had a herd of goats and he agreed to sell me a week's supply at the time. The noise my family made as I poured goats milk on the cereal was horrendous. They hated the sight, sound and smell of it and it was banned from the house.

I had always made my own brown bread and we continued to have that as well as lots of fruit and vegetables. If anyone complained they hated a particular vegetable I just shoved it in the blender with the gravy and poured it on their dinner. I made soup until it came out of our ears.

I continued to sneak goat's milk in to the house as I had discovered that I could make my own yoghurt in a big vacuum flask. As long as I mixed it with lots of flavourings nobody realised. I knew that my children hated the fact their home made packed lunches were different to their friends.

Mr Green, the teacher, who was organising the trip to Germany lived next door to us and agreed he would keep an eye on Theo. There is a certain feeling that ripples through a crowd of parents whilst they are waiting for the return school trip. The sight of the coach coming round the corner and your child's smiling face is a joy to behold. Theo bounced off the coach and could not wait to tell us he had lived a whole week on sausage and digestive biscuits. His allergies improved as he grew but I know that time when he could not play rugby or football really affected him. His extra time in the classroom though was well spent as he began to excel academically.

CHAPTER 102
Leg Warmers and Aerobics

When family life is very busy the outside world news tends to take a back seat. I loved music and The Police and Tom Petty were my current favourites but the children's tastes began to permeate the house. Fame was very popular with Miranda and Irene Cara's voice could be heard being played loudly.

Leg warmers were very popular in our house with both mother and daughter. I started to go to aerobics at the town hall with my sister and all the girls from work. Our red faced exertions knew no bounds as we threw ourselves first this way and that.

Gillian and I nearly had apoplexy one day as we drove past my boss Vivienne. She had dashed home from a meeting, yanked on her leggings, pulled on her trainers and decided that the mile walk would do her good. As we passed her, Gillian screamed "Oh No Vivienne's got her knickers sticking out of the back of her trainer."

We screeched to a halt and called her over. We asked her whether this was a new sartorial look or an unintentional consequence of a speedy change of clothes. By the time we arrived at the town hall we were all hysterical.

I loved my little blue mini and would have kept it forever. We had decided that it would be better if Gillian had custody of it during the week. She had further to travel than me and I did not mind the walk to work. She collected it on a Monday morning and brought it back on a Friday evening.

That Saturday morning Grant jumped in the car shouting "Come on we are all late." We all jumped in he put his foot down and reversed out of the drive onto the quiet road on which we lived. The look on his face moments later was priceless. The next thing he shouted was, "Who the hell put that there?"

There was steam coming out of the engine and steam coming out of his ears. As we piled out of the car I surveyed the scene and got the giggles and that set the children off. Grant made two phones calls that morning. He made one call to the garage to collect his smart new car for repair and one to the scrapyard to collect the mini that was no longer a mini.

He was absolutely convinced that it was my sister's fault. She had parked the car on the road outside the house instead of on its proper place on the drive, the more irate he got the more hysterical I got. It was only when I had stopped laughing and gone in to make a cup of tea that I realised I had lost my only form of transport. The year ended sadly with the news that John Lennon had been shot and was dead. On the 8th of December 1980 John and Yoko Ono had been returning to their New York apartment in the Dakota. Mark Chapman shot John Lennon four times in the back. John was taken to the emergency room but he was pronounced dead on arrival. Yoko Ono issued a profound statement:-

"John loved and prayed for the human race. Please pray the same for him." I was stunned by that news. Like most people of my generation I loved the Beatles. However it was John's haunting voice that was the sound of my youth. Even now when I hear his voice it brings a lump to my throat.

CHAPTER 103
The Royal Wedding

Charles and Diana got engaged in February 1981. The country rejoiced and when they announced the wedding would be in July I said to Gillian "That is a short engagement". She replied, "You silly woman, it's not like they have to save up like the rest of us."

It was planned to be on July 29th that year and it just so happened to be James's 6th birthday. He loved writing letters and regularly wrote to my aunts in Canada. He asked me if he could write to Prince Charles and Lady Diana and I helped him compose the letter. I was really impressed by the swiftness of the pleasant response. I asked him not to mention this to his grandma as she still considered anything royal, "a load of old tosh".

Mother was very confused and hurt at this time because her political heroine had deserted the Labour party. In March the "Gang of Four" consisting of David Owen, Roy Jenkins, Bill Rogers and Shirley Williams had left Labour because they thought it was too "left wing". Mother had admired Shirley Williams, daughter of Vera Brittain[*] for years. She admired her style. The news that she had helped form a centre party was a surprise. They formed the Campaign for Democratic Socialism which would be known as the Social Democrats.

Shirley Williams had lost her Labour party seat in 1979. She was the first Social Democrat president in 1982 and then became leader of the Liberal Democrats in the House of Lords. The Liberal Democrats were formed in 1988 by a merger of the Liberal Party and the Social Democrats. The Liberals had been in existence for nearly 130 years before the merger.

In March I went on strike for the first time in my life. I could not really avoid it. In a small town everyone knows your business and everyone knew that my father worked for a trade union. It was a national strike but only about a third of the office stayed out.

On a lighter note the children and I watched The Eurovision Song Contest and thought that Bucks fizz were worthy winners with "Making your mind up."

Theo had fortunately overcome his allergy problem and played in cup winning team of the Kendal Cup. He was doing well in school and appeared to be very happy. Miranda loved horses, ballet was far behind her and she spent every weekend at the local stables. She was there every school holiday and loved being out in the fresh air. She was also very good at tennis and doing well academically.

James's main complaint was that he had to spend all his time with mum and dad whilst the others got to do exciting things. He never got it into his head that he was four years younger than them. He wanted to do what they did whatever it was.

When he was 13 yrs old and the others were out partying he had his last New Year's Eve alone with us. Grant, James and I were watching Columbo and I had just nodded off. I awoke to a loud yell, "I cannot do this anymore, I hate staying in." He was so upset but he only had to wait 15minutes and there was a clamour at the front door. It was his brother with about 20 friends who had come back for something to eat. They ate me out of house and home that night.

· Vera Brittain, a writer, feminist and pacifist was the author of *The Testament of Youth*. In this she recounted her experience in the First World War and her journey towards pacifism.

CHAPTER 104
The Stories of the People with the Best Views

In April I did something else that I had never done before. I conducted the census. I have always loved "magic money" an unexpected windfall and I have never, ever minded having to earn it. Years later I worked each year at the Money Mail Advice Centre at the Ideal Home exhibition. I loved looking round and trying to decide.

The delicious sense that this money has no purpose is not earmarked for anything and has freedom to choose without guilt. That was what doing the census meant to me. I had a census lesson, signed the secret code and was given the census forms. As a serving civil servant I was considered one of the suitable people.

At that time you actually knocked on the door, took the form in the house and filled it in with them. You were paid a certain amount of money for each house and you had to do it in a certain amount of time. I was startled to find that my patch was the swishiest area of the Lake District. The only trouble was that the houses were miles apart.

The first door that I had the temerity to knock on was a beautiful mansion. The door was answered by a maid. She showed me upstairs to see the lady of the house. The upstairs sitting room had the most beautiful view of the lakes and the mountains. The lady of the house invited me to take tea. Whilst we sipped lapsing souchong and filled the form in she told me her amazing life story.

So it continued, long winding drives and all human life behind the front doors. I leant on kitchen counters, knelt in gardens and sat in the back of chauffeur driven cars whilst I got the information the form required. That does not happen anymore but it was a very interesting experience in human nature. I actually put the "magic money" towards a new car but that was alright.

CHAPTER 105
I am Afraid We will not be at The Street Party

A street party was to be held in honour of the Royal Couple. I said that I would help organise it but I was not sure that we would be able to be there. We had spent all out money on some remodelling and so we were going to have a caravan holiday. Grant's sister and her husband were keen caravan people and they had kindly agreed to lend us their van. Grant had a tow bar fitted and we made plans. We had never towed a caravan before and to say I was concerned was an understatement.

The journey in the rain was uneventful. As we approached our destination Bude in Cornwall the rain just got more intense. Some wag in the back of the car was heard to remark that wherever we went we seemed to take the Lake District with us.

As we got out of the car James remarked in a querulous voice as he surveyed the scene, "Mummy where is the hotel? " I explained to him that we would be staying in the contraption that we had dragged 350 miles behind us.

He burst into tears, "Mummy I thought we had brought that thing just so we could have a cup of tea on the motorway." As I stood in the pouring rain looking at my husband struggling to secure and make level the dratted thing on a sloping site I thought "What we have done.?"

The views we had been promised were there we just we couldn't see them because of rolling mist. We were cold, wet and fed up when we climbed into bed that night. I say climbed but it was more of a slide sideways and then flops into bed in the confined space.

The next day dawned clear and so we followed the family motto. "Don't mope, get out and see what is happening." It was a jolly bunch that made their way to Clovelly that morning. If you have ever been to Clovelly then you will know it's a picturesque, very steep road down to the beach. The only way back up is that same picturesque steep up road up again.

Whilst deciding what to take on holiday in that very small caravan I was in a quandary. I had actually stood with my sandals in one hand and my trainers in the other hand weighing them up like the scales of justice.

I had plumped for my sandals and left my trainers on the bed. We had a lovely time looking in the shop windows as we meandered down the steep slope. I did wonder if my sandals were the correct footwear.

As we stood on the beach the bad weather began to roll in again. One minute I was standing on a rock and the next minute I was not. My stoical self had never ever experienced such agony. I had slipped off the big rock and landed on the little rock and the pain made my head spin and I did not care who knew it. When I looked down my foot was going black and my big toe was definitely going sideways and I was sure I was facing forwards.

Grant said through gritted teeth" we will just have to make our way slowly back up the hill. "Are you mad," I screeched. "I would rather die lying here on the beach than attempt that climb" - "My big toe is going in an entirely different direction to the one I am going in." A kindly local stopped, "There is a Land Rover kept in that shed for emergencies."

The driver of the Land Rover was summoned and my wide eyed children accompanied me in a stately procession up the winding road. Theo and Miranda slid down in their seats because they were so embarrassed by their mother who had managed to draw attention to her again. Only James enjoyed the ride waving at everyone we passed. Grant had to run behind as there was no room for him in the Land Rover. Through the red mist of pain I decided I was secretly glad he had to run behind as in my opinion he had not been sensitive enough to my predicament.

When we got back in the car he drove straight to the hospital. The handsome young doctor there wiggled my toe back into place. Ignoring my screams he suggested that we buy a pair of green flash pumps three sizes larger than my foot and keep it on until we got home and could seek medical care.

This man had just got hold of my foot. Was he blind could he not see how big it really was? They did not make green flash pumps in three sizes bigger than my enormous feet. He did however prescribe me some codeine for the pain.

The children were starving so we bought fish and chips and they fell fast asleep when we got back to the caravan. I spent the night drinking brandy and silently weeping. I must finally have fallen asleep when I heard a clanking noise outside in the mist. It was Grant moving about. As he disappeared and the reappeared in the gloom I said "What are you doing?"

"Going home" he said "I really, really cannot take anymore." We piled the children in their pyjamas into the car but with the traffic it was early afternoon by the time we got home. We all looked frightful. Miranda, Theo and James were in their pyjamas, Grant exhausted, and his hair was sticking up and I was definitely past my sell by date.

As we staggered out of the car 40 expectant faces beamed up at us. It was the Royal Wedding street party and everyone shuffled up so that we could join them.

CHAPTER 106
W Marched in London

In October of that year I did the third thing I had never done in my life before I joined 250,000 people on a CND march in London.

I travelled to London with mother, father, my sister Gillian and her best friend Julia.

I made sure with the children and Grant that they were happy for me to go for the day. When they answered in the affirmative I made my plans. There was a palpable air of excitement on the train that day. We had sandwiches and drinks in our back packs and it was one of the only times in my life that I saw my sister in flat shoes.

When we caught up with the rally we were amazed to see how many people were there. The rally actually took more than five hours to wind its way around the centre of London. When we arrived in Hyde Park to listen to the speakers I looked around at all the different types of people there. As I had walked along chatting to fellow marchers I had been a little nervous of punk rockers with their safety pins. I found that the kids with blue Mohicans were just as nice as any other people. I learned a big life lesson that day about not judging people by their appearance.

The speakers were all interesting. Tony Benn wanted to close the air bases and Michael Foot rejected the insanity of nuclear weapons. Father seemed to know many people and introduced us to a lot of Labour politicians.

It was a very long day but we felt our participation had been worthwhile. It was also great to spend the day with our parents. CND The campaign for nuclear disarmament was established in 1958 at the height of the cold war. It was at its most popular in the 1980s with 100,000 members. In 1998 CND membership had dwindled to 40,000 members.

We had a lovely family Christmas that year and all the children put on a show. The two littlest boys sang a song but insisted on holding hands and facing the wall whilst they sang to avoid embarrassment. They were still doing that in their teens. Mother was in great form that year and it was good to see her enjoying her grandchildren.

CHAPTER 107
Is That Man in the Poncho Please to see Me?

We planned our summer holiday early the next year. We intended to push the boat out a bit and really enjoy ourselves. We were still at that lovely stage of family life where it's all for one and one for all. Children did their homework when they were asked and turned up to the meal table smiling.

The faintest sound of slammed doors and answering back was barely discernible in the distance. You could only hear it if you put your ear to the ground and listened very carefully. We decided on Portugal and booked a villa in the grounds of a fancy hotel in Albufeira.

The day of the holiday arrived and we set off in high spirits. The journey from Manchester Airport was faultless and the children enjoyed flying. Music was changing and the older children liked Depeche Mode and Teardrop Explodes as well as Michael Jackson.

THE FOURTH GENERATION

As we were shown to our villa we were very impressed and nodded a greeting to our next door neighbours. We went for an obligatory meeting in the foyer the next morning. The holiday representative said in her pitched sing song voice " Portugal is a very safe country, very little crime," She went on to tell us that if we wanted to get the best rate exchange for our pounds into escudos then we should use the local bank.

After offering us a warm glass of cava she disappeared into the distance. We sat down to have a cold drink and make a plan. We decided to walk the mile into town to change our money and buy a few groceries. As we walked it began to get hot and I was glad that we had put sun lotion on the children and made them wear hats and sun glasses.

As I peered into the distance I was glad when I saw the shops appearing. We were chattering away when I saw what looked like Clint Eastwood standing outside the bank. As we strolled along the thoughts drifting through my mind were, "I bet he's very hot in this weather in that woolly poncho." I like his hat, he looks like a cowboy. Why is he shaking that big stick at those people?"

At that same moment Grant and I both realised that the big stick he was shaking was a rifle and he was shouting the Portuguese equivalent of, "Get in the bank now otherwise I will blow your head off." When shocking things happen to you time slows right down. Somehow Grant grabbed James and I pushed Miranda and Theo behind me.

We ran for the door next to the bank which was a bar. They had already called the police and shocked people stood around talking. We really had no idea what was going on but managed to calm the children and get them a drink. The next thing we heard was a shot and the robbers came running out of the bank. They all were wearing ponchos which made it very easy to spot them. The police arrived in the one police car they had followed by several officers on push bikes. There was a lot of running around and shouting and then the hostages came piling into the bank. Most of them were the English people who had been at that fateful welcome meeting that morning. They were in front of us because we had stopped for a cold drink.

THE FOURTH GENERATION

The Portuguese bank manager had flatly refused to give money to the robbers. Even when he had been threatened with the gun shot, which had brought down part of the roof, he absolutely refused to comply with their demands. Then they decided to rob the customers. The people who had not been served lost their watches and wallets, but the poor people who had been served lost all their cash as well.

The police kept us in the bar for hours whilst they interviewed everybody. The language barrier was a real problem. We had French, Spanish, German and Italian between us. The only Portuguese word the polite English people seemed to know was "Obrigado". Most people seemed to be waving their hands about and mouthing "Clint Eastwood" when they were interviewed.

CHAPTER 108
Has Mother been on the Vino Verde?

A s we arrived back at the hotel complex and made for our villa we noticed that there were police there as well. The family in the villa next to us were from Yorkshire and had been to the beach that morning. When they arrived back at their villa they realised that they had been robbed. They were understandably very upset and the police closed off that part of the hotel complex.

About five families were moved from that part of the hotel including us and we got a very welcome up grade.

As we sat down to enjoy our evening meal we decided to try out the much recommended Vino Verde. That went down very nicely and so we ordered another bottle. James read the name on the label and pronounced it "Possip".When I tried to stand up I had a little difficulty. I blamed the heat, the stress and anything else I could think of. The children clapped their hands with glee and announced that their mother was definitely " Possiped." As I lay in bed looking at the stars through the velux window I thought to myself "Ha! So much for crime free Portugal"

CHAPTER 109
A Delicious Meal on the Beach

In fact the rest of the holiday went really well. There was a lovely swimming pool and the children spent hours in there. We had always insisted that the children swam with t-shirts on in the heat of the day and that worked for a while.

When a new pool attendant came on duty she insisted that they could not swim in t-shirts. It was against company policy. I thought that was a really crackers idea but my Portuguese was not up to the argument. We had all decided to give the holiday company rep a miss as she seemed to be a source of flawed information.

That evening we walked along the beach and found a picturesque restaurant. It was early so there were not many people about. They ran out to show us the catch of the day and invited us in. It was delicious but the problem was that when the bill came it was more than we expected. I do not know what we thought but it was not the exorbitant amount that constituted about half our holiday money.

We discussed it between ourselves and realised we had no alternative but to pay up. As we walked home we decided that we should probably stick to holidaying in countries where we could speak the language.

We spent the rest of the holiday on the beach. The water was clear and clean. The boatmen came in to shore with grapes and melons and the family played lots of beach volley ball and tennis. We had a trip to Spain and as we sailed across the river on the ferry Grant leaned across to me and said "This is the only time this ever going to happen to me". I frowned at him quizzically and then it dawned on me. My 5'10" husband was a head taller than any other man on the ferry. We had a delicious lunch and then got the afternoon ferry back to Portugal

Later on Grant made a pronouncement. "I am never going to Spain again in my life" He had been suffering from tummy ache all evening and blamed the Spanish lunch.

I reminded him of those years later during the five years that we spent living in Spain. We hired a mini during the last few days of that holiday. As we drove over the brow of a hill looking for a restaurant James spied an orange grove in the distance and asked if his dad would stop. We were all grateful to stretch our legs. We were lolling about chatting and discussing oranges. I was explaining to the children that citrus trees cropped twice a year and so you could see flowers and fruit at the same time. I have no idea if that is true; I just thought I must have read it somewhere.

CHAPTER 110
A Large Dog and two Metal Cars

I was stunned into silence when my daughter let out a bloodcurdling scream. All our eyes followed her pointed finger and realised that a very large ferocious looking black dog was heading down the hill. If we had been in a competition that day we could not have got back in the mini any faster. As Grant who had been shepherding us in like a demented policeman finally slammed the door the dog screeched to a halt beside us. We never discovered if he was friend or foe as we were too busy putting some distance between us.

That holiday had not finished with us yet though. As we waited at the airport we decided on balance that we probably would not visit Portugal again. What happened in the next few minutes made me wonder if we were ever going to be able to leave? James followed me through baggage control and I helped him lift his ruck sack on the conveyor belt. As we were getting organised I noticed that the man with the scanning machine was putting James's bag through again and again. As I bent down to tie the lace on my trainers I felt the air around us sizzle with action.

When I lifted my head up over the conveyor belt I realised that we were surrounded by armed police. Something in James's bag had set all the alarms off. The senior policeman pulled on white gloves carefully and opened the bag with trepidation. At this stage the whole airport had stopped to stare at us. I had already picked my small son up and was holding both him and my breath very tightly.

Then there was a peal of laughter as the policeman pulled first one and then the other small metal car from James's bag. The cars had been lying at right angles and looked to the man as though they might be a small gun .With much amusement we were waved on our way. We decided on the plane that we really would never go to Portugal again.

CHAPTER 111
Learning To Canoe

The rest of the summer was spent getting Miranda ready to go to senior school. Theo was spending the last week at scout camp and Grant hired a mini bus to take them up to the Langdales. Grant had trained a canoe instructor and helped with the camp.

Whilst Miranda and Theo were at junior school they had a wonderful teacher called Mick Jones. He was an amazing man who only had one eye but was totally fearless. He lived just across the road from us. He taught scores of children, including ours, to abseil, rock climb, fell walk and canoe. I was grateful for all the time he took out of his family life to do this. I know what this entailed because his wife was a friend of mine.

Our children spent two weeks every summer at the YMCA day camp. There they learned to be fearless. This was especially important to me for Miranda. I had grown up frightened of everything to do with trusting my body. I trusted that my mind would cope but not my body. I wanted her to be free as a bird. To be able to climb, run and jump. During my grammar school education I had been given an opportunity to learn how to do many things. They offered trips to listen to the Hallé Orchestra, to learn to ski and on field trips all over the world.

I never took the letters home thinking that the family could not afford it. My sister did though and she went to France, Germany and Italy on school trips. The rules in my head had dictated that my family could not afford the trips. I do not know why as both my parents worked. My mother met a neighbour once and asked her if I was going on the school skiing trip. When she asked me about it I said, "I didn't bring the letter home as I thought we could not afford it." That evening I basked in the glow of my parents pleasure at having such a selfless daughter.

THE FOURTH GENERATION

I made myself a promise then that my children would be able to do anything and everything. I wanted them to soar as high as they could in life. I also wanted Miranda to be able to change a wheel and the boys to be able to cook and iron a shirt!

CHAPTER 112
Can Anyone Tell Me what a Teenager is, Please?

"A person whose age falls within the range of 13-19 whose age number ends in teen"

Your life is wonderful. You love your children, your husband, your extended family and your job in that order. You look in the mirror and the clear eyed woman looking back at you has a knowing look in her eye. She is in control.

"Oh no you're not, Oh yes I am, Oh no you are very definitely not." I was very definitely not ever in control again for years. There should be warning, there should be a sign, and there should be something. A something that warns you that your precious child has turned into a TEENAGER. The problem for me was that my beautiful, clever daughter Miranda and my wonderful, handsome son Theo turned into teenagers the very same night.

I did not know that morning at breakfast that nothing was ever going to be the same again. When I look back there were signs. Theo, 13 yrs. who everybody remarked looked like a young Elvis, had perfected his snarling lip movement. Miranda 12 yrs. had developed a terrifying thousand yard glare and her lips were constantly pursed. Only my darling 8 yr. old James, with his bright blue eyes chatted, away whilst eating his shredded wheat.

By that time in our lives I really believed that I could do it all. I knew I had MS. It was the relapsing and remitting kind. Grant had agreed with my decision not to tell anybody as I did not want people feeling sorry for me. I was strong and capable and I always believed my mind could over-ride my body. If I had a bad spell then I covered by saying it was migraine or flu.

I was the local authority appointed chair of a board of governors of a large school. I was also a member of the PTA of all the children's schools. I was working hard at work and had passed exams which meant I had a promotion. I also did not need more than about four hours sleep a night so I had started an Open University degree.

Grant met the children from school that evening and it was his turn to cook supper. As I pulled up on the drive I could hear the first of the many cataclysmic arguments that would characterise the relationships between my two oldest children.

I now realise I should have raised my voice above the din and asserted my authority and sent them up to their rooms. I missed my chance that day. I had treated them like precious jewels and was in awe of them but teenage brains have changed out of all reason and a different approach is needed.

Teenage brains are different from children's and adults brains. A friend described it to me as, "an entertainment centre that is badly wired and does not have a speaker."

There are all great kids who became powerful and amazing adults but all my intellectualising and acquiescing was not the right approach. However my innate gut feeling and all that I had read about parenting in the1970s told me then that my approach was the correct one.

Chapter 113
My Husband's Mother

My mother-in-law Laura was a star during those years. She had been a widow for about a year when I started work and had come every summer ever since to help with the children. We took on every holiday with us because she loved seeing new places and the children were now used to her rather brusque ways.

Her marriage to Francis had been very volatile. She loved her childhood sweetheart with a passion but he was not great at being responsible. She was also much cleverer than him and he resented that. He was an only child of a very strict father who had expected more of him. Frank senior, who had risen to the dizzy heights with Co-op, lived every day in disappointment.

Francis was a was a large bear of a man who towered over his diminutive father. He was great at making everyone laugh or hiding crisps under his shirt for his grandchildren but he was hopeless with money.

Laura had scrimped and scraped when her children were young but in later life found a job in a bank at which she really excelled. When Francis died everyone expected her to get on with her life. She had always been very independent. She was fifty six years old when she became a widow and everyone included her daughters, her sisters and her friends were very unsympathetic.

Ten years before her husband died she had miscarried at seven months pregnant the day she came out of hospital she had to go straight to her daughter's wedding and she had not had time to grieve. She spent many hours at our house after she was widowed and talked endlessly about the little boy she had lost.

CHAPTER 114
Steamed Puddings and Poker

Laura was a good plain cook and so in the school holidays were filled with pies and puddings. She was strict with the children and played endless games of cards with them. Grant joked that his mother was teaching them to be card sharks and my mother was teaching them to be good socialists. Mother and her sister Beth did not agree about much but they did agree about Greenham Common.

In December 1982 30,000 women joined hands around the Greenham Common base. This was called the "Embrace the Base" event and my mother and aunt were amongst the women there.

Laura was entirely different to my mother even though they had grown up in the same area at a similar time. Laura really did not understand Mona's view of the world. The rules and regulations that had to be obeyed confused Laura, "Just relax and sit down," she said. She loved Barbara Cartland and Rosamunde Pilcher and could still be found reading a 2am. She also loved breakfast television that had recently started broadcasting. She loved the fact that she could watch television whist she drank her coffee whilst my mother thought it was a waste of time.

They did agree though on their feelings about Margaret Thatcher. The employment figures released in February were at 3.2

million the highest that they been since the 1930s. They had been through the depression as children. They shared folklore was that the worst thing you could you could do to a man was take his job away. The idea that a man was the head of the house and it was his job to keep his family was still prevalent in their thinking. When Mrs Thatcher was re-elected in June by a landslide there was much tut tutting in my parent's house. My mother actually stopped speaking to her neighbour across the road over the election. This dreadful woman (who was actually a friend of mine) had the temerity to put up a Conservative Party poster in her front window. Mother was convinced that as the whole neighbourhood knew her politics and so should have respected her feelings before they put the poster up.

This made me want to collapse in fits of giggles but I waited until I had driven off the drive before I did. She also spoke very rarely to her next door neighbour as they had built an extension and could see in her kitchen window. The policeman's family next door seemed very nice even though I did not know them well.

Years later, after my mother had died I was standing at the bottom of her garden, heartbroken and weeping. I felt someone's arms around me who held me whilst I sobbed. When I finally composed myself I looked up expecting to find an uncle or a cousin and found myself looking into the eyes of Paul, the policeman from next door. I will always be grateful to him for reaching out that day.

CHAPTER 115
How Do You Decide what You Decide?

I had known from childhood that I the ability to make people feel better. My grandmother Hester had always said "You have a face that people tell things to and it will be a curse and a blessing." What I did not have was a filter to stop other peoples woes becoming my own. So the problems of the world just piled up on my shoulders. I was a news junkie and suffered with the poor and the mistreated. Father had always said "If you asked you all your neighbours to put their troubles in a pile in the middle of the road, you would take a look and pick up your own up." He also said when I was small and complained that I could not see my skin because of the psoriasis, "Be lucky you have you have legs to stand on"

I really had absolutely no sense of the importance of self as a separate entity. I knew what I wanted for my children, my husband, my family and the world but in common with many women I had no idea what I wanted...

I wish someone had explained to me then that it is not healthy to keep saying "Yes" to everybody all the time about everything. You cannot say "Yes" in a vacuum. When you say "Yes" to one thing, you say "No" to another. When you say "Yes" you will finish work report before morning, you are saying "No" to a child that needs to speak to you now. When you say "Yes" to a middle aged parent that wants to live with you in your house, you are saying "No" to your husband who does not really approve. When you say "Yes" to a teenage boy who wants to take your car on a 800 mile trip you are saying "No" to peace of mind for a week.

If people pressure you for an immediate answer you can say, "If I have to give you an immediate answer, then I am afraid it has to be "No." You do not always have to be a nice guy and if you continue to be one then you are then you are storing up trouble down the line. The light at the end of the tunnel may be a steam train coming in the other direction I wished I had known all that then.

The trouble is that although life can be reviewed backwards it has to be lived forwards. I had lots of confidence. That was not the problem. It was just a sense that I must endure whatever was thrown at me. When I married Grant I said to him, "Whatever you do I will always forgive you." I knew that I meant that. Early in my marriage I had complained about something trivial to mother. I will never forget her words. "I endured, what makes you any different." My advice to my younger self should have been: Take your time when making a decision or tackling a problem. Make sure you step to one side and consider:-

Position 1.Look at yourself and really see what you are thinking and saying. Check how this makes you feel.

Position 2 Look at the other person or point of view clearly. Put yourself in their shoes for a few moments.

Position 3. Imagine you can see the whole picture that is unfolding. From your lofty position consider the whole situation for a while

This is called Stepping to third and gives you great perspective. Then make your decision with clarity and purpose.

CHAPTER 116
The Biggest Extension on the Block

I did not know any of this as 1983 drew to a close. The family seemed to be settling into a new routine. We were becoming 5 separate entities rather the tight unit of the early years. I knew in my head that young people need a sense of freedom but in my heart I was finding it very hard to loosen the ties.

One of the problems that faced us then was that we needed one more bedroom. We already had four bedrooms but always seemed to have a lot of visitors. I did not think it was fair to move one our growing children out of their bedroom for the summer when my mother-in-law came to stay.

Grant said to me one morning as he passed, "I know we need an extension." I nodded my head whilst frying mushrooms for the ever hungry mouth that was the slow cooker. Excitement and ambition coloured our judgment and our plans grew increasingly grandiose. As our architect neighbour looked around I found myself asking him to draw up plans for 2 more bedrooms, 2more bathrooms, a playroom, a second sitting room and a utility room. As Grant and I stood chatting after the architect had left we thought how wonderful it would be to have more space.

CHAPTER 117
Is This 1984?

"It was a bright cold day in April, and the clocks were striking thirteen"

Published in 1949 George Orwell's dystopian novel introduced the watchwords for a life without freedom "Big Brother is watching you." The main character Winston Smith wrestles with oppression in Oceania, a place where The Party scrutinises every action".

In January of that year life for our family was going very smoothly. Grant and I were very excited about the plans to make our home much larger. The children seemed to be finding their feet in an increasingly grown up world.

Miranda had grown early and was now a beautiful young woman. She was now taller than her older brother and never let him forget it. After a great academic start at her new school she had dipped at the end of last term and I was worried. I knew the headmistress of the school well as I was involved in fund raising as deputy of the Parent Teachers Association. I made an appointment to see her and asked the blunt question "What has happening with my daughter's education?"

"Well, she's got brains, that is for sure." She pulled out the list of all the exam results for the year Miranda had gone up to secondary school. As she ran a beautifully manicured nail down the list she stopped at no 12 of a hundred plus children. " Happens with girls at this age, some stay in the guides and some don't," she said with a shrug of her shoulder. "Make sure she is in with the right friends," were her last words.

Grant and I sat in his car outside the school talking deciding what to do. We were adamant that we wanted all our children to go to university but we were not sure about a heavy handed approach. I let out a snort of laughter when I thought about Miranda's exit from the guides. The trouble was that she had always had the ability to make me laugh and I found it impossible to stay cross with her for long.

Last month, Helen the guide leader had given a month's exclusion to two girls for misbehaving. One was Miranda and one was Janine. Helen told me this with chagrin as Janine was her daughter. When I mentioned this to Miranda she flounced out saying, "I am a bit too big for singing round that particular campfire anyway." Miranda had carried on the family tradition of supporting the underdog and she was not afraid to voice her opinions to anyone. She had a skill which cannot be taught, you either have it or you don't and

Miranda had it in spades, you know when you think, "I wish I had said that to them." Well my daughter already had said and moved on.

When she was 8 yrs. old and her little brother was 4 yrs. old I was called into school. That lunch time Miranda had looked out for James to make sure he was alright, as she always did. When she spied him standing on a chair she flew across and demanded to know what was going on.

It transpired that the dinner lady had imposed the punishment on him for spilling his peas on the floor. She lifted him off the chair, told him to carry on with his lunch and rounded on the dinner lady." How dare you treat my baby brother like that, it is disgraceful." With that she went back to her seat.

The elderly headmaster explained this story to me with raised eyebrows. The trouble was that Miranda was his favourite, no contest. "Whatever are we going to do with her,?" he said beaming from ear to ear.

I was not really comfortable with Miranda's best friend Ella. She lived across the road from us and had a lot of freedom. I liked the family and knew the mother well. However she did not seem to obey the rules. Whilst I was peeling potatoes preparing three course meals she let her children help themselves out of the fridge. I did not have a high opinion of that.

CHAPTER 118
I am Always Peeling Potatoes

I have a picture of myself in my mind's eye. I am wearing a beautiful pink and purple silk scarf across the shoulders of a cream cashmere sweater. I have on a knee length straight skirt and navy high heels. My thick brown hair is cut into a sharp mid length bob. My makeup is immaculate and I am smiling at something I have just heard on Radio Four. "She definitely is not a control freak," I say to myself, "but she could pass for one in a dim light."

My meals were delicious and contained the correct amount of vitamins and minerals that growing children needed for health. I knew that because I had done the research. We always had a soup to start chicken, mushroom, vegetable or minestrone. Then a main course meat or fish with a choice of three vegetables with sauces, I was good at sauces. Then a steamed pudding, isles deflottantes or a raspberry trifle. I had no idea who made the rule that said I had to spend two hours cooking like that every night. I was one of the few mothers who worked in 1984. In the back of my mind I regarded my career as self-indulgent and standing doing the dishes at 9pm was my punishment.

My eldest son asked me years later why I had fed them like miners to walk round the corner to primary school. I thought, "Cheeky beggar, it didn't do you any harm. You are brainy as can be and 6 ft. 3 in to boot." In hindsight I was as wrong about that as I was about many things. As we sat in the car that day after meeting Miranda's headmistress Grant and I talked about our daughters' friends but decided just to keep an eye on the situation.

My other concern was the school. The system in our area had changed from the 11 plus to comprehensive education five years before. I agreed with comprehensive education intellectually but I really thought the system was in some chaos. They were still testing the children but they went to the local school based on which one was closest to their home.

I explained to Grant my concerns about education at that time. We were both involved in education as school governors and we read every paper that came out about education. I have great admiration for teachers and think they do an amazing job. A wonderful teacher can change the trajectory of a child's life. That year however was a time of real unrest in education. Most teachers had stopped doing anything that was not in their contract. That meant no after school clubs which really affected the children.

There was also a laissez-faire attitude prevalent. I was walking down a corridor one day and heard two teachers talking, "I would not advise any kid to become a teacher, it's a terrible occupation" I thought, "I hope no child heard that." The conclusion that we came to do that day was that we would mention this visit to her. We decided to offer her the opportunity to go to a private all-girls school that was about 10 miles away. I had already spoken to the headmistress and she thought there was a place for Miranda.

Two things stopped me sending her to that school. She shouted and raged at me that she did would never, ever leave her friends. The other thing was that I knew my mother would have a fit because she was absolutely against both private medicine and private education.

As Grant got ready to drive off he said, "The most important thing is that she becomes herself." As I climbed back into my car and watched him drive away I was heard to mutter, "As long as she graduates that is."

Of course she did go to University and met her wonderful husband of twenty years there. The subject she chose for her degree was Women's Studies. Of course if I had known that then it would have saved me years of worry.

CHAPTER 119
The Squished Tomato

With the wonderful gift of hindsight I made a mistake about Miranda's education. I should have sent her to the public school. She was clever, funny and popular. She also had a brother who was exactly one year older than her who had a mind like a steel trap. Anything that ever went in stayed there for ever. He was also really well behaved and good at every subject.

I know that it really got on her nerves that he appeared to be so perfect. Two weeks after starting primary school he was given the responsibility of looking after a little boy who had had a stroke.

A month after he started at senior school we found him in the garage late one night. He was sawing an old kitchen cabinet in two. "There is a boy at school who is blind and people keep moving his things," I said. "I would make him a cabinet to keep them in." I looked into my sons green eyes and realised that I had handed him the mantle of "Keeper of the world."

I cannot say I ever saw Theo carrying a school bag. He would just sit at the back of the class and listened to what the teacher was saying and it went straight into an uncanny ability to pass exams. His biology teacher wanted him to be a marine biologist but he had dreams of the City even then. The first time I ever saw him write an essay was when he was doing his MBA in France and we had gone across to visit him.

THE FOURTH GENERATION

Theo's best friend was a charming local boy who became a charming man. I always thought Blake was perfect even when I had evidence to the contrary. He was a great footballer and added a sense of fun to Theo's life. He also had a friend called Jonathan. His mother and I went to lots of evening courses together. We made jewellery, learned French cooking and abstract painting. She was newly divorced from an older man and just had one child. When I think about those years, she was always away on some trip or other so Jonathan was always with us.

One morning I was in the village store which sold most things. It was also a post office and I was busy sending a letter to Canada. I had five children with me. Theo, Miranda, James, Jonathan and my niece Claire. For absolutely no reason that I could think of 7 yrs. old Jonathan decided to climb up and over the high screen in front of the post mistress and fling himself down on to the other side. She screamed loudly at the same time as the girl in charge of the shop yelled. When I looked back, my niece who was in the push chair had buried her face in pounds of ripe tomatoes. They were squashed in her mouth, her hair and all over her brand new pram.

It took us a while to extricate ourselves that morning. I had to look after the shop whilst the assistant went to make a cup of tea for the post mistress. She had come over with the vapours and needed to sit down and I of course had to pay for the tomatoes. As I walked back up the hill I wondered to myself if other women had lives like mine. I rolled my mouth around the word "No" to see how it felt.

CHAPTER 120
My Blond Little Boy

My youngest child held my heart in his hand. Blonde with bright blue eyes he was gorgeous. I knew a few weeks after he was born that he was to be my last child. I had been really ill after he was born and so we made the decision not to have another child. We decided to appreciate the children we had, rather than worry about not having more.

THE FOURTH GENERATION

James was just perfect; when he smiled the sun came out. Being in his company made you feel better. Everyone still feels like that about him now even though he is now the father of delightful sons himself. The only time I have ever been cross with him was in his "Ned's Atomic Dustbin" years. I had asked him to wait for the holidays to have his hair cut. He was at a strict boarding school and that year his holidays started before the other boys. When he arrived home I could not see the problem as his hair seemed to sweep back. He smiled and flicked his head and his fringe fell to one side to reveal a completely shaved head. I am ashamed to say I flew down the hall to the front door and tried to clock him with whatever was in my hand. The incident ended well though because he was a foot taller than me and much faster and my instrument of choice was a tea towel. I asked "What if they expel you?" His answer fascinated me, "I can play rugby and pass exams, what are they going to do?" In 1984 James was still at primary school and enjoying every day. .   He went everywhere with his best friend Richard and they were like two peas in a pod. Both had an older brother and sister and we were good friends with his parents. The father William came from a "well to do" local business family and the mother Sue came from Liverpool. She fascinated our children because although she spoke with a very posh voice she swore like a navvy.

We did not allow swearing in our house and to hear these "expletive" spoken loudly in Received Pronunciation was just too much for them to bear. James was at that lovely age for boys when all that matters is climbing, shouting and playing football. Boys tend to be nicer to each other for far longer than girls. Life for boys at 8 years old tends to be fancy free. He was really happy at this time in his life.

Years later I went to meet my oldest granddaughter from nursery. I think she was just three. As she was walking towards me, an even smaller girl approached her and whispered in her ear. Amelia shrugged and ran into my arms. I said to her" What did that little girl say to you darling?" She thought for a moment and then said, "Oh, she said she did not like my boots."

CHAPTER 121
The Miners' Strike, Thatcher and Madonna

Every single item of news in that year began with the letter M. It was the Miners' Strike, Margaret Thatcher or Madonna. The Miners' Strike began in March 1984. Their leader Arthur Scargill dominated the union and opposed the Conservative government led by Margaret Thatcher. The strike was precipitated by Thatcher's appointment of Ian McGregor the previous year. He had previously run British Steel where he halved the work force in a year. Mrs Thatcher had been re-selected in June 1983 by a landslide. She saw this as a complete vindication of her monetary policies. She believed that government had no place running business and began selling off state assets.

In March 1984 the National Coal board announced that it intended to close 20 coal mines with the loss of 20,000 jobs. All the miners went out on strike, except for Nottingham. The government was prepared and had stock piled coal and had begun converting coal power stations to oil.

The strike became increasingly bitter. Miners picketed en masse and there was intimidated at work pits and coal depots. The government began mobilising large squads of police to stop the strikers. There were lots of violent battles. The Battle of Orgreave in June saw 5000 strikers and 5000 police fighting pitch battles.

The Conservative Government decided that as local police forces may well be sympathetic to their neighbours, they would send in deployed offers from other areas. Strangers were more likely to challenge the striking miners. The police officers often camped out in the area. The strike proved a watershed for UK industrial relations. Mrs Thatcher called the strikers "The Enemy Within" and insisted the rule of law must prevail.

Arthur Scargill continued to promote the strike and as money was very short, hunger became rife in the mining heartlands. The strike was nearly a year old when it finished in March 1985. The unions had become very powerful in the 1970s and 1980s. The defeat of the National Union of Mineworkers proved to be the turning point in the power of the unions.

My parents were very upset with what was happening to the miners at this time. A neighbour was a form teacher for one of my children. In class that morning she had ranted about the terrible thing the miners were doing to the country. My son put his hand up and tried to put an opposing view. She became incandescent with rage and sent him to the year head for punishment. When my child explained what had happened the year head raised his eyebrows, smiled and said, "Sit in the Library for 10 minutes, go back and apologise and then sit down." He finished with, "There is no right answer to all of this."

A lot of different things happening as 1984 rolled on but it was all to the soundtrack of Madonna's music. Her hits were Borderline, Holiday, Lucky Star and Material Girl. However her rendition of Like a Virgin was deemed to be shocking and went far too far. You definitely thought that it was too far especially if you were the mother of a teenage daughter who wanted to dress like Madonna.

Fortunately Miranda preferred Tracey Ullman and played "You broke my heart in 17 Places", especially the track "They don't Know" over and over again.

CHAPTER 122
You Can Have Your Bat Back young Man

I was really enjoying my job but suffered from "mothers double guilt."   A mother feels guilty that she is not a good mother because she is a work.

The consequence of that was that I ran around all the time. Mother said to me "For goodness sake girl stop running around you will meet yourself coming back". The rules stated that I had to make my own bread, grow my own flowers, change the bed linen every week and cook Cordon Bleu meals.

A mother feels guilty that she is not a good employee because she always has to run out when her children need her.
The consequence of that was that I worked harder than anyone else. I had to prove my worth and in a corner of my mind I fancied another promotion.

THE FOURTH GENERATION

One weekend I asked Grant to pick some raspberries for tea. The raspberries were growing wild at the bottom of the garden. The only trouble was that there was a 6 foot fence between him and the raspberries

He asked, a child that shall remain nameless, to hold the bottom of the ladder whilst he climbed over with the bowl I had given him. The child wandered off, the ladder tipped up and he went over the top. Whilst managing to keep hold of the bowl he twisted both ankles. Theo who by this time was as strong as an ox manages to get his dad back over the fence. We spent the rest of the afternoon in A&E. When I got back my mother rang as she had cut her hand and father was away. I jumped in the car picked her up and went back to A& E. Fortunately this time I had taken a book.

The next morning I was just getting out of my car at the office car park. A woman called Judith who insisted on cycling everywhere had fallen off her bike. As I helped her into my car she was crying bitterly. "Are you OK?" I said sympathetically. "No," she wailed, "Just look at my tights."

I said down to wait in reception, thinking it was my third visit to casualty in eighteen hours. That is the last thought I had though because when she finally came to get me I was fast asleep, lying across 3 chairs snoring softly.

My husband could no longer play squash with his friend Dennis who was a lecturer at Lancaster University. He was complaining one night and all I heard was "squash, squash, and squash". I mentioned this to the girls next day and the following week I was the proud recipient of a voucher for a squash lesson for my birthday

They were all good players so they left work early to come with me. The court had a mezzanine level from where they could watch me have my lesson. I looked up and waved at the four jolly figures. Since I could walk I have known that my brain does not reach my feet. After about 15 minutes I looked back to see my friends and they were not there. As I was looking back thinking, "miseries they have gone." I saw two hands slowly followed by a face appear. Eventually all four faces appeared, bright red and breathing with difficulty. They were all laughing so hard they had fallen on the floor.

I turned my gaze back to my handsome instructor and he was laughing hysterically as well. With as much dignity as I could muster I handed him my bat and left the court.

CHAPTER 123
I Really Need a Hobby

We had our planning permission and D day was Theo's birthday. My quantity surveying trained husband had looked at the figures and decided he could build this monstrosity himself. Grant, Harry and Malcolm each had a lump hammer and were beginning to bash the concrete garage. Every time one of them bashed the hammer it just bounced off the pebble dash. There was much discussion about angles and weight ratios and I had to go in because they were knocking my house down.

They did however get going and within two weeks they had laid the foundations but it was not without pain. Grant had taken a school party water skiing four weeks before I had broken two ribs. The injury was compounded by a cheery note from the new headmaster attached to a photo. It was of Grant water skiing and the note said" First case ever recorded of under water skiing.

I could see Grant was struggling with laying the concrete and asked him if he had asked his son to help him. He nodded at the window and through the blinds I could see Theo peering back at me. It was not like him he was always so keen to be involved with his dad's projects. I remember thinking, "Gosh he doesn't look happy," but the thought disappeared from my mind like a wisp in the wind.

The extension slowly took shape. Grant worked every hour to get it ready for the brick layers. We were so lucky that summer as it did not rain for weeks. His Uncle Fred had been a master brick layer and came to supervise the men. It was so exciting coming home to see what had been done.

The problem was it was all much more expensive than we imagined. The roof tiles arrived one sunny morning. There were thousands of them as it was a very big sloped roof that the architect

THE FOURTH GENERATION

had designed. I went in to make a cup of tea and when I came out he was still staring at the tiles.

He looked so forlorn and when he said, "I have got something to tell you," my heart missed a beat. "Let me sit down," I said as I slumped on to a garden chair. "What is it?"

If I had taken a thousand guesses I would never had got it right. As I looked out over my beautiful garden he looked up and said, "You are going to have to tile the roof."

CHAPTER 124
The View From The Roof

Grant then went on to tell me we really could not afford a roofer. We would both have to climb out on the roof and as he cut each tile I would have to nail it into place.

In my life I had done a lot of gardening and painting but didn't he know I had vertigo? He assured me I would be held on by a rope. My lovely holiday that stretched out before me was spent on the roof. Every morning I climbed up a tall ladder and he followed me up. In my shorts, sunglasses and big hat I laid thousands of tiles. I ruined my manicure that fortnight but the funny thing was we talked and talked as there was nothing else to do.

I discovered that my husband was really bored with his job and wanted a change. He was 36 years old and wanted to make his mark in the world. I stared out from my eyrie to see my family in the garden. At 9, 13 and 14, they were really growing up. I knew they were going to enjoy living in this lovely big house.

I had to learn lots of other skills that year. We finished the outside before the autumn rains came. Then we worked late into night finishing inside. I plumbed in bathrooms, painted walls and did emergency plaster work.

I spent that summer and autumn feeling that all was well in the world. At Christmas we had a great big party to celebrate finishing the house. We all danced to 1999 by Prince from his Purple Rain album. You know when you get that feeling that sends tingles down your spine. A view, a touch, a moment: I had that feeling that night. My family were happy, every room in the house looked amazing and I hoped we could stay in this house forever.

It was Grant's birthday the week after Christmas. He mentioned to me he had a meeting in London on that day I did not think any more about it. He was staying the night and would be back the next afternoon.

I was taking the Christmas decorations down when I spied his car on the drive. All my married life I have always gone to the door to say goodbye and all my married life I have always gone to the door to greet him.

So I was standing at my beautiful new oak door when my world spun on its axis. He was holding an enormous bunch of roses and lilies. I knew it was his birthday not mine so why was I getting flowers? I looked at his face and knew he was going to tell me something important. I smiled a greeting and went to the drinks cupboard. The first thing I saw was the sherry and so I poured myself a large glass of the amber liquid.

CHAPTER 125
I Cannot Hear What You are Saying

Grant was speaking to me. I knew that he was speaking because his mouth was moving. I just could not hear a word he was saying. Whatever it was I did not want to hear the words. I felt unbidden tears squeezing out of the corners of my eyes. My brain screamed "Do not do this to me, whatever it is, I don't want to hear it" I took a sip of the sweet, sickly liquid. It tried to make its way down my closed throat. I took a deep breath and opened my eyes.
" Hello love, did you have a good day?"

He was so excited; he had been offered an amazing job by the directors of the oil company that he worked for. I set my face into a smile and went to hug him. Over his shoulder I looked furtively at the clock I did not want my children to walk in on all this.

We had always had a policy of being honest with them. If something was going they knew about it, whatever it was. I knew once they came in this news would be out and I saw that I had about half an hour to get the details.

He ran to get a bottle of champagne from the spare fridge in the garage. Whilst I waited for the pop of the cork a thought entered my frozen mind. Life was never going to be as good as it is now. My children are doing well at school. My life is a wonderful thing. I looked around at my lovely home and saw a photo of the Christmas party with everyone's smiling face. I liked my job and the office was only two minutes away from everything if there was an emergency.

My thoughts were interrupted by a cold glass of champagne suddenly arriving in my hand. As he started to speak my eyes were drawn to the icy moisture on the outside of the glass. I knew I had to compose myself and listen.

He would have more responsibility; more status and he would be managing lots of people. His title would be Managing Director of the subsidiary oil company that he was going to run. He came over and put his arms around me and swung me round. As he kissed me he whispered in my ear, "I really want to do this."

I could hardly form the words to my question as my mouth was so dry and I knew deep in my heart that I was not going to like the answer. He put his head down and did not look at me "400 miles away in East Anglia". I never got a chance to reply to that as the children came rushing in and the news was out.

Grant had booked a restaurant so we could all talk. I hardly ate a thing as I looked at my children's faces. James did not care as long as he was with his dad. Miranda loved an adventure then just as she loves one now. I could not see how Theo was feeling as he would not meet my gaze. The company had given Grant until the next day to decide whether he wanted the job. In that restaurant, that night the decision was made to go to the exciting new life.

A life has to be lived forwards and can only be reviewed backwards put my fears into the back of my mind and went to tell my mother I was taking her grandchildren 400 miles away from her.

She stared at me with her pale green eyes under her rather severely cut fringe. "We have had ten good years living near each other and you must know nothing is for ever." I had expected her to show some emotion, and I burst into tears and flung myself at her slight frame. She did what she always did, she patted my back and she said what she always said, "This will pass like everything else."

I went to the park and had a good cry for so much that had happened to me in my life. Who had made these rules that I had to obey? More importantly why did I always obey them without putting up a fight?

CHAPTER 126
Stop That Car Immediately

The next day I was driving past the cinema with James. We had "Shout" by Tears for Fears" on the radio. The road becomes straight there and there was not much traffic about. I started to put my foot down. Suddenly without warning a car swerved in front of me and screeched to a halt. I slammed my brakes on. It took me a moment to realise I knew the driver who was advancing towards me with his face as red as his tie that was flapping in the wind. He signalled with his hand that I should wind the window down. Leaning in with his face inches from mine he shouted, "How dare you?"

"How dare I what Dad?" – "Your mother tells me you are upset about having to move house. Your place is with your husband, always has been, always will be. Behind every successful man is a woman who makes it her life's work to support him. Support your husband and don't upset your mother again."

"You alright Mum," said James as we set off again. As I glanced across at him I could see he was shaking his head. Grant told his company that he would take the job and began to formulate a plan.

He would go at Easter and stay there during the week. Neither of us could bear to sell the house we had worked so hard on so we decided to keep it. It was a safety net in case he hated his job or the children did not settle.

We decided that we could just about afford to buy another much smaller house near his new office. We considered that the most important thing was the children's education so we needed to find the best school.

Today everything is on line and schools have league tables but then it was all guess work from 400 miles away.

THE FOURTH GENERATION

Miranda had a French teacher who had taken her on a school trip and I knew he had taught in the area so I went to see him. He recommended the school he had taught at and so we started our search there. Grant was travelling a lot at first and so we decided to leave our search for a house until the summer holidays.

That left me on my own with the family for a few months. I asked my manager if I could work part-time to be around for the children. "Part time" was frowned on and he shook his head. I went back into my office and Barbara said "You know I am not far off sixty and I would love to work less. How about we share a job?" We worked out the details and went back to him with a plan.

We would each work a week handing over on Wednesday lunchtime. He nodded and then said pompously, "It will take you at least two hours to hand over and you will do it on your own time not mine." I agreed and ran out of the room. I would have agreed to anything to get more time with my children.

Life settled into a rhythm and Miranda and James were looking forward to the move. I did not realise it then but Theo at 15 years of age was at that exquisitely difficult stage of life between boyhood and manhood. He had grown very broad and his shoulders were very wide. He was still waiting for his growth spurt and was smaller than most of his friends. I wish I could have told him then that by the end of that summer he would be 6'3". He had a northern accent and he was much cleverer than everyone he ever met including his teachers.

His behaviour began to change quickly after his dad started his new job. He was miserable and sullen and when I tried to hug him he pulled away. I knew deep in my heart that moving him was probably not a good thing. What could I do? The train had already left the station. Grant loved his new job, the pay was much better and an exciting new life beckoned us.

That summer was my mother's 60th birthday. I spent weeks organising her day. She did not like any kind of surprise especially parties and so we decided it would just be her children and grandchildren. The day dawned with great news. My brother was to be a father again and this would be her 8th grandchild

I had planned something for every hour. We had breakfast out and when we got back the photographer had arrived to memorialise the day. We had lunch by the Lake and went to a show. We ended the day with very tired small children in a restaurant. I walked my two nephews around and around the car park as they were so full of sugar they were just bouncing about.

A week later it was time to go house hunting in East Anglia. Theo flatly said "I am not spending a weekend looking round houses. I will move when you move but I am not coming now." I asked my mother if Theo could stay with her overnight whilst we were away. She nodded her head without looking at me. I walked around, captured her gaze and held it. "If you agree to do this for me I need your assurance you will not give Theo the key to the house." She smiled at me, "Mum please he is a 15 year old boy with lots of friends. I cannot go unless you promise me that you will not give him the key." She nodded her head" I will not let him have the key to the house"

CHAPTER 127
The Long, Long Night

We set off in good spirits with our youngest two children and sang all the way down the motorway. Princes "Raspberry Beret" was the favourite. We had dropped Theo off at his friends with the promise that he would sleep at grandma's house. It was a sunny afternoon when we pulled into the grounds of the hotel where we staying.

The children went for a swim and then they served us a cream tea in the garden. Miranda and James went in to watch television and Grant and I enjoyed a walk in the evening sun. He held me tight and said "it is all going to be alright you know"

We had just finished a delicious dinner when I said, "I better go and check in with mother and make sure Theo is there." Father answered the phone and I could not get the gist of what he was saying. I asked him to slow down so I could understand what he was saying.

"Theo persuaded your mother to give him the house key. Every teenager in town is in your house and it has got out of hand. The police are there and now the fire brigade have arrived. What do you want me to do?"

What did I want him to do? What did I want him to do? I was 400 miles away. I could not believe my parents had given him the key. I put the phone down and ran to tell Grant. This was at a time when we had answer phones but mobiles had not been invented.

He rang our house and the answer phone kicked in. "Theo pick up phone, pick up the phone now." By the time the tape finished he was screaming like a banshee but Theo still did not pick up the phone. He was crying when he said to me." How could we have left him, he is only 15 years old." I realised then that he was not angry with him, just scared that he was alright. He reserved his anger for what he described as my crackers parents, "How could they have given him the key?" The first thing we did was ring the local police and explain the situation. The first thing they did was assure us that the house was not on fire but the fire brigade had been called out by a prank call. They still had a presence at the house but it was beginning to calm down. They had scores of complaints from the neighbours. We said we would be back as soon as we could.

We had a restless sleep and then set off at 4 am. Grant drove like the wind and we were back before breakfast. As we drove up to house I could see cans and bottles in the garden and the road. I could see neighbours peering out of their windows. There he was sitting on the sofa all alone. My lovely Theo was alright that was all that mattered. We decided there and then that house would have to be sold and we would buy a family house near the school in which we had enrolled the children.

As we cleaned up after the party that morning the phone never stopped ringing. Every parent whose children had been at the party wanted to talk to me. Every neighbour had a complaint and my relationship with my parents was definitely much cooler.

CHAPTER 128
A New Life is Beginning

At the end of the summer Theo went with his dad to start his new school. Grant was not letting his oldest son out of his sight. Miranda, James and I followed six weeks later. I had sold the house and we had bought a new one. It looked lovely and to my delight had an acre garden. The house had been built the year before and the garden was a muddy field. I knew I was going to have time to tend it as I was not going to work for a year.

I had spoken to the manager of the office where I hoped to work. "I don't allow my staff to work part time" he said" you can start tomorrow if you want to come back properly. "I was really upset but once I had thought about it I was grateful as I wanted to spend time with the children and continue with my Open University degree. Also to be honest my symptoms were getting more pronounced. I definitely had a limp and was feeling excruciatingly tired. When I thought about it the rest and fresh air were properly going to be good for me.

First of all though I had to pack up possessions and leave my family, friends and work colleagues. On that fateful morning as the removal van moved off down the road I turned to hug my parents, brother and sister, nieces and nephews farewell. I looked at all the little faces with tears streaming down them. My heart was in pieces. As we drove away I waved my arm in goodbye and I caught sight of my watch. I noticed the date and realised that it would have been my great grandmother Hannah's 100th birthday. As I bade her silent hurrah I wondered what she would have made of the woman her great granddaughter had become.

THE END

Footnote

Although we kept that house for seven years we only lived there for two years. Grant got another promotion to London and decided to take it and move everyone again. It became our weekend home and we enjoyed the garden.

Grant climbed the ladder of success before having a heart attack at 50.yrs. He slowed down and is now fit and well. I went to work in the Press Office in London before retraining as a Psychotherapist. I enjoy being grandmother to seven amazing people.

Mother died in her early sixties and my heart still breaks every time I think of her.

Father is still alive in his nineties and regards every day as an adventure. All that cycling when he was young means he can still run up the stairs.

Gillian became a headmistress and then retired to Spain. She has 3 grandchildren.

Harry chose a career in education. He is amazing with children and takes his 4 grandchildren everywhere with him.

Miranda studied Women's Studies at university and met her future husband there. They love travelling and now they take their amazing children with them wherever they go.

James went to university to study economics and now has an amazing career in London. He still keeps in touch with every friend he ever made. His boys are as wonderful as he was when he was little.

Theo stayed in education until he was 25 years old .He got married the week after he came back from university in France. He is a powerhouse in the City and has three wonderful children.

Two of Hester's daughters are still alive in Vancouver and all the extended family keeps in touch. I am sure Hester would be delighted by the many wonderful descendants she and Frank produced.

It is going to be alright in the end and if you can't hear the wonderful lady singing in the background then it's not the end.

***

Lightning Source UK Ltd.
Milton Keynes UK
UKOW06f2349130516

274220UK00001B/14/P